THE SPINOZA CONVERSATIONS
BETWEEN LESSING AND JACOBI

Text with Excerpt from the Ensuing Controversy

GERMAN LITERATURE, ART & THOUGHT

AN INTERNATIONAL FORUM FOR INTERDISCIPLINARY STUDIES

including *The McMaster Colloquium on German Literature* Vol. III ff.

Published by University Press of America
Lanham, London, New York

Edited by Hans Schulte

Associate Editors: Peter Heller and Gerald Chapple

ADVISORY BOARD

THE SPINOZA CONVERSATIONS BETWEEN LESSING AND JACOBI

Text with Excerpts from the Ensuing Controversy

Introduced by
Gérard Vallée

Translated by
G. Vallée, J.B. Lawson, and C.G. Chapple

UNIVERSITY
PRESS OF
AMERICA

anham • New York • London

Co-published by arrangement with
German Literature, Art & Thought, McMaster University

Library of Congress Cataloging-in-Publication Data

The Spinoza conversations between Lessing and Jacobi : text with excerpts from
the ensuing controversy / introduced by Gérard Vallée ; translated by G. Vallée,
J.B. Lawson, and C.G. Chapple. p. cm.
Translated excerpts from: Die Hauptschriften zum Pantheismusstreit zwischen
Jacobi und Mendelssohn / hrsg. und mit einer historisch- kritischen Einleitung
versehen von H. Scholz, 1916.
Bibliography: p. Includes index.
1. Lessing, Gotthold Ephraim, 1729–1781—Philosophy. 2. Lessing, Gotthold
Ephraim, 1729–1781—Religion. 3. Spinoza, Benedictus de, 1632–1677—
Influence. 4. Pantheism—History—18th century. I. Jacobi, Friedrich Heinrich,
1743–1819. II. Mendelssohn, Moses, 1729–1786. III. Vallée, Gérard, 1933–
IV. Scholz, Heinrich, 1884–1956. V. Title.
PT2415.H38   1988   832'.6—dc 19   88–21091 CIP
ISBN 0–8191–7015–1 (alk. paper)
ISBN 0–8191–7016–X (pbk. : alk. paper)

FOREWORD

Die Hauptschriften zum Pantheismusstreit zwischen Jacobi und Mendelssohn [1916] [The Main Writings Relative to the Pantheism Debate Between Jacobi and Mendelssohn], presented and introduced by H. Scholz, remains the best collection of documents pertaining to the controversy which shook the self-confidence of the German Enlightenment at the end of the 18th century. I am presenting here in translation significant sections of this documentation, including Jacobi's famous account of his conversations with the late Lessing. The selection of passages has been governed by my estimation of what contributes best to the understanding of the issues at stake, and of what is most instructive as to the understanding of Lessing and the unfolding of the controversy. The Introduction aims at providing the context of the debate and takes into account recent studies of "Lessing's Spinozism", with the hope that it does not merely repeat well-known analyses but also offers a perspective able to manifest anew the fruitfulness for the present of a not so old debate. The reader will be able to test the validity of that perspective against the translated texts which so well display the character of the participants.

For many reasons, some more obvious than others, I soon abandoned the idea of offering a translation of all the documents assembled by Scholz, especially of Jacobi's extensive footnotes and long excursus. The obvious reason resides in the fact that the hundreds of hours required for such an enterprise were simply not at my disposal. A further reason is found in my fear of hiding the forest for the trees. For my area of interest is defined by the question of Lessing's "Spinozism" and that, only to the extent that such a question is relevant to the understanding of Lessing's own work. While this initially constituted Jacobi's interest as well, the course of the pantheism controversy led him more and more to switch his focus and to devote himself to more general problems such as the nature of philosophizing, the dangers of rationalism, the pitfalls of nascent idealism. Given my own area of interest, I felt justified in not translating here many of Jacobi's further additions which aimed more and more at his own self-justification. But translating only Jacobi's report of his conversations with Lessing would not do either; more is needed if one wishes to understand the context in which they took place as well as the context of the pantheism debate. Therefore, not all of Scholz' text is included here, but what is included is substantial. I do hope, however, that somebody will one day offer a complete translation of these documents as well as of Jacobi's other relevant writings. It would surely fill a sad gap and make the ideas of perhaps the most valuable critique of the Enlightenment directly available to English speaking audiences.

If the translation offered here attains a certain degree of accuracy and fluency it is largely due to the expertise of two colleagues in the German Department at McMaster University: C.G. Chapple and J.B. Lawson. Over a year I shared with J. Lawson dozens of instructive and pleasant "Morgenstunden," revising my initial translation in order to make it "capable of travelling"; then the three of us together established the final text.

My introductory essay considerably profited by the perceptive criticism of friendly readers whom I thank wholeheartedly here. I have a special debt of gratefulness to Ms. Barbara Bayne for her patience and competence in editing the Introduction and revising the translated texts.

Research for the entire work was made possible by a Leave Fellowship and a Research Grant I received from the Social Sciences and Humanities Research Council of Canada in 1985-1987; for both awards I wish to express here my renewed thankfulness.

McMaster University
Hamilton, Ontario
August 1987

CONTENTS

ABBREVIATIONS AND CODES

GW Lessing's *Gesammelte Werke*, edited by P. Rilla.

LM Lessing's *Sämtliche Schriften*, edited by K. Lachmann and F. Muncker.

LY *Lessing Yearbook.*

ThLZ *Theologische Literatur Zeitung.*

Werke Lessing's *Werke*, edited by H.G. Göpfert et al.

WSA *Wolfenbütteler Studien zur Aufklärung.*

ZThK *Zeitschrift für Theologie und Kirche.*

CODES for notes and footnotes:

In **Introduction:**

[51] In the text of the **Introduction** refers to the pages of **Texts** translated below.

In **Texts:**

1 changes from Jacobi's first edition, or Scholz' footnotes.

* Jacobi's footnotes.

[=] my own additions [most of the time in the text itself].

INTRODUCTION

The Spinoza Conversations Between Lessing and Jacobi

Lessing's Spinozism looms up out of the numerous intellectual riddles of the past. Almost everything has been tried in an effort to sound and weigh the exact amount of Spinozism Lessing betrayed in his conversations with Jacobi. The findings could hardly clash more resoundingly; some say that Lessing was a resolute Spinozist; others, that he was not more than a mitigated Spinozist; that he only had vague leanings toward Spinoza; or that he had secretly devoted himself to Spinoza from the beginning; or that he never took his Spinozism seriously; or that he contradicted Spinoza on central points; that his sporadic interest in Spinoza should not be used to give a general interpretation of his thought. It seems that all shades of interpretation of Lessing's Spinozism have been expressed: from total denial of any substantial relationship to the tracing of almost every idea of Lessing to his reading of Spinoza. In fact such variety on this specific point is but a reflection of the most contradictory interpretations of Lessing's overall position, according to which he was either a theist or a deist, an atheist or a neologist, a rationalist or an orthodox Lutheran, deeply religious or indifferent to, or making fun of, religion, a good-natured heretic, or however one feels inclined to name him.[1]

To some extent Lessing's Spinozism bore the quality of a self-inflicted *nemesis*. In conversation with Jacobi, Lessing had declared: "If I am to call myself by anybody's name, then I know none better" than Spinoza [85].[2] Without paying due attention to the conditional limitation of the statement or to the general difficulty

---

[1] For the baffling diversity of views on Lessing see J. Schneider, *Lessings Stellung zur Theologie vor der Herausgabe der Wolfenbütteler Fragmente.* 's-Gravenhage 1952, pp. 7-15.

[2] References given in the text are to the pages of the translated passages below.

of encapsulating Lessing's thought in a short formula, interpreters rashly applied the label "Spinozist" to Lessing and justified such application by "his own words." More often than not, the label "Spinozist" not only meant any anti-establishment stance but it also meant "atheist" and could well be used to discredit a person. This fateful turn has been taken by many critics since Lessing's death; the result has been a tarnished reputation. Indeed Spinozism has been the Trojan horse introduced into Lessing's works to shake the citadel of his thought. In the 1950s the suspicion reached the ears of a large English-speaking audience due to H. Chadwick[3] and his presentation of Lessing the "rationalist."

The wonder of it all is that, in spite of all his ambiguities, or rather because of them, Lessing has continued to. fascinate us.[4] His talent for raising the right questions remains unsurpassed. His searching ways nourish our own quest. If we consider the continuing discussion about Lessing's Spinozism in particular, it is simply not correct to call such a discussion fruitless;[5] it has already forced interpreters to weigh Lessing's utterances concerning Spinoza, as well as any of his statements, against the entire canon of his writings and thus enabled them to reach a better grasp of his literary production. This is no small contribution.

Furthermore, it has to be recalled that the historical efforts to interpret the statements Lessing made to Jacobi [the "Spinoza conversations"] were responsible for launching the pantheism debate of the late 18th century, one of the most significant debates for the emergence of a modern view of the world and one that considerably shook the self-confidence of the German Enlightenment; in that debate Jacobi thought he had demonstrated that, after all, the basis of the *Aufklärung* resided in a questionable mixture of downright atheism and vague nature-piety. The pantheism debate is full of respectable efforts undertaken by

---

[3] H. Chadwick, *Lessing's Theological Writings*. London 1956.

[4] As a sample of that fascination we name only two authors, well apart in time: S. Kierkegaard [*Concluding Unscientific Postcript*. Princeton 1941, p. 67: "Aye, one seldom finds an author who is so pleasant to have to do with as Lessing"] and H. Arendt [*Men in Dark Times*. New York 1968, p. vii; she does not hesitate to treat Lessing as a contemporary, and a most attractive one at that].

[5] As claimed by R.R. Heitner in *LY* IV, 1972, p. 199.

worthy thinkers with a view to shaping a concept of reason that would not exclude religion and morality from the realm of intelligibility. We can still learn from it.

When related to Lessing scholarship in particular, however, the Spinoza conversations cannot be innocently considered as the undisputed key-text for the interpretation of Lessing. This questionable hermeneutical step has been taken, though, and repeatedly, by those interested in disqualifying the Enlightenment in general and Lessing in particular with the bogey-word, "Spinozism".[6] The present essay attempts to show how problematic, at least how delicate, an operation it is to read the casual statements of the late Lessing back into the entire *corpus* of his works, including his earlier works.

1. Lessing's Conversations with Jacobi

When Gotthold Ephraim Lessing died on February 15, 1781 at the age of fifty-two, he left behind an amazing collection of writings cast in almost all literary genres and often showing a rather unconventional character. Indeed such variety in his literary production was intentional. At the age of twenty he had written to his father about his "inclinations to try [his] hand at all kinds of

---

[6] The many weapons of ancient heresiology, from loud invective and abusive rhetoric down to wicked maligning, seem to have all been mobilized against Spinoza during the century following his death, as documented by D. Bell, *Spinoza in Germany from 1670 to the Age of Goethe*. London 1984, esp. pp. 1-23. It is not surprising that Jacobi's broadcasting of the news about Lessing's Spinozism was perceived as an outrageous disgrace. To be fair to Jacobi, it has to be recalled that his intention was not "to libel Lessing" nor, for that matter, "to convert Mendelssohn", as some suspected; he was, rather, intent on discrediting the rationalism of the *Aufklärung*, as Bell correctly says [p. 85]. To be totally fair to Jacobi, however, Bell should also have emphasized the fact that the debate made of Jacobi one of the main agents of the Spinoza-renaissance in the 1780s.

poetry."[7] His inclination became embodied in epigrams, songs, odes, didactic poems, fables, parables, stories, theatre plays, literary critiques, letters, philosophical and theological essays and pamphlets. Undoubtedly the interests of the philosopher-poet covered a wide range, and if one wishes to find fault with them one can suggest that maybe they did not extend to a due appreciation of music, of landscape, of romantic love. Yet these possible shortcomings were overwhelmingly compensated for by an unusual mastering of Antiquity, vast readings, and robustness of argumentation. Among the "brood of songbirds" of the German literary circles of his time, with whom he condescended from time to time to exercise his voice, Lessing has been rightly seen by Dilthey as the "young bird of prey"[8] who finds special delight in teasing the songbirds and challenging the habits of the nest; in so doing Lessing revealed the full measure of his abilities while helping German literature toward the realization of its mature state. The days of the polyhistor might have been numbered; yet Lessing was certainly one representative of that species of universal scholar, perhaps among the last.

Shortly after Lessing's death Moses Mendelssohn expressed his intention of "writing something on the character" of his lifelong friend.[9] In fact we know of an outline that Mendelssohn probably wrote in the early Summer of 1781.[10] But the real *laudatio* was only to appear in his *Morgenstunden* [Lectures xiii, xiv, xv]: it will have turned in the meantime into an ill-concealed apology of Lessing.

Meanwhile Friedrich Heinrich Jacobi heard of Mendelssohn's plans through Elise Reimarus,[11] a close friend of Lessing in his

---

[7] Letter of April 28, 1749 in *Werke* II. München 1971, p. 598.

[8] W. Dilthey, "G.E. Lessing". *Das Erlebnis und die Dichtung*. Leipzig/Berlin 1919[6], p. 26.

[9] Letter to Karl Wilhelm Ferdinand Herzog von Braunschweig, Feb. 20, 1781 in M. Mendelssohn, *Gesammelte Schriften*. Vol. 13, p. 5. See also letter to J.G. Herder, May 18, 1781 in R. Daunicht, ed., *Lessing im Gespräch*. München 1971, p. 577.

[10] In Daunicht, *Lessing*, pp. 577-580.

[11] Letter of March 25, 1783 in H. Scholz, ed., *Die Hauptschriften zum Pantheismusstreit zwischen Jacobi und Mendelssohn*. Berlin 1916, p. 66. While Scholz presents all the essential documents relative to the controversy between Jacobi and Mendelssohn concerning Lessing's ultimate creed, preceded by an important essay on the

late years. Elise was the daughter of the famous Hermann Samuel Reimarus whose sensational essays in Biblical criticism had been published posthumously by Lessing and who, on that occasion, had been revealed as the secret initiator of the German Enlightenment. The "trustee of the most precious legacy" of the *Aufklärung*,[12] Elise R. functioned in the present situation, with more or less success, as the go-between in the exchange that brought Jacobi and Mendelssohn to blows at times quite unfriendly.

At the news of the impending publication of Mendelssohn's "something on Lessing's character," Jacobi got nervous. He was probably anticipating that Mendelssohn, in his encomium, would call in Lessing as a witness in favour of his own rational theism; he might also have anticipated that crucial elements of Lessing's real thought would without doubt be glossed over. At any rate, Jacobi was firmly convinced that he understood Lessing better than Mendelssohn did. He therefore decided to reveal to Elise R. some of the contents of the conversations he had had with Lessing a few months before Lessing's death, expecting that she would relay them to Mendelssohn, which she did.

> You know perhaps, and if you do not know I confide it to you here *sub rosa*, that Lessing in his final days was a firm Spinozist. It is conceivable that Lessing may have expressed this view to others; in that case it would be necessary for Mendelssohn, in the memorial he intends to dedicate to him, either to avoid certain

---

controversy, A. Altmann, *Moses Mendelssohn. A Biographical Study*. The University of Alabama Press 1973, pp. 553-759 contains a minute presentation, in chronological sequence, of all the details of the unfolding events. For his part, H. Timm, *Gott und die Freiheit. Studien zur Religionsphilosophie der Goethezeit*. Vol. I: Die Spinoza-renaissance. Frankfurt/M. 1974 offers an impressive study of the constellation of ideas of the years 1780-1790, out of which Lessing's legacy kindled spectacular sparks; his work is devoted to the Spinoza renaissance and the Spinoza debate which informed the "philosophy of religion of the time of Goethe."

[12] H. Blumenberg, *Arbeit am Mythos*. Frankfurt 1984[3], p. 450.

matters totally or at least to treat them with the
utmost caution. [79][13]

The unexpected news could not fail to disturb Mendelssohn to
the utmost. He asked for more information, always through the
agency of Elise R. On November 4, 1783 Jacobi sent Mendelssohn
[via Elise] a substantial report of his conversations with Lessing, a
report that was intended as proof of his statements to Elise to the
effect that Lessing had become a Spinozist; the report was to
kindle the debate on pantheism that voiced the first major
challenge to the German Enlightenment and left its mark on all
German philosophy of religion to come.[14]

What then had taken place in the course of the encounter
between Lessing and Jacobi that was so inflammable? What did
Jacobi reveal in the report of his conversations with Lessing? As

---

[13] Letter of July 21, 1783. In his introduction to *M. Mendelssohn, Gesammelte Schriften*,
Vol. III, 2, p. xvi L. Strauss interpreted Jacobi's intimation as a "trap" designed to
embarrass Mendelssohn; in fact, the latter did react the way Jacobi had wished. Now it
can be granted that there was something awkward or even clumsy about Jacobi's
initiative; but I find it exaggerated to presume, as Strauss does [p. xxx], a lack of
sincerity in Jacobi's communication.

[14] There followed many letters between Jacobi and Mendelssohn in the course of what
became a rather ill-fated relationship. Loud protestations of mutual respect and
expressions of excessive politeness go side by side with an almost continuous lack of
real communication. At times it becomes very difficult to distinguish between mere
misunderstanding and intentional deceit in the dealings of these two strong but touchy
individuals. The outcome of such uneasy relationship was that, in 1785, practically at
the same time and without explicit consultation, Mendelssohn published his
Morgenstunden oder Vorlesungen über das Daseyn Gottes [Morning Lessons or Lectures
on the Existence of God] and Jacobi, his *Über die Lehre des Spinoza, in Briefen an
den Herrn Moses Mendelssohn* [Letters to Herr Moses Mendelssohn on the Doctrine of
Spinoza] containing the report of his conversations with Lessing and letters exchanged
with Mendelssohn. Shortly before his death Mendelssohn defended Lessing's theism in
*An die Freunde Lessings. Ein Anhang zu Herrn Jacobis Briefwechsel über die Lehre des
Spinoza*, 1786 [To the Friends of Lessing. Appendix to Herr Jacobi's Correspondence on
the Doctrine of Spinoza]. Finally Jacobi justified himself in *Wider Mendelssohns
Beschuldigungen in dessen Schreiben an die Freunde Lessings*, 1786 [Against
Mendelssohn's Accusations in his Writing to the Friends of Lessing]. The essential parts
of those four works constitute the *Hauptschriften* presented by H. Scholz.

Jacobi arrived in Wolfenbüttel on July 5, 1780 for his *first* personal encounter with Lessing, he carried among his papers a poem by the young Goethe, the "Ode of Prometheus," that was to become the ominous starting point of the conversation. The next morning, while putting final touches to this correspondence, Jacobi handed the poem over to Lessing with the words: "You have so often given offence that you will not mind taking offence for once." [85]

Goethe's poem consists of a monologue by Prometheus, which Goethe later thought could have opened the third act of his planned drama.[15] Prometheus the Titan stands here as the symbol of rebellion against the established order; he opposes the world despot, Zeus, seen as depriving humans of their divine freedom, and, defiant, asserts his own creativity and autonomy; while concerned with the lot of humans, he is unable to see, in the injustice of destiny, a loving providence.[16] Here is the poem.

PROMETHEUS [1773][17]

Cover your heaven, Zeus,
With cloudy vapors
And like a boy
Beheading thistles
Practice on oaks and mountain peaks -
Still you must leave
My earth intact
And my small hovel, which you did not build,
And this my hearth
Whose glowing heat
You envy me.

I know of nothing more wretched
Under the sun than you gods!
Meagerly you nourish
Your majesty

---

[15] For a discussion of this presumed destination of the poem, see H. Fisher-Lamberg, *Der junge Goethe*. Bd. III. Berlin 1966, pp. 437-438

[16] See Timm, *Gott und die Freiheit*, p. 183.

[17] Translation by M. Hamburger in C. Middleton, ed., *J.W. von Goethe: Selected Poems*. Boston 1983, pp. 27-31.

On dues of sacrifice
And breath of prayer
And would suffer want
But for children and beggars,
Poor hopeful fools.

Once too, a child,
Not knowing where to turn,
I raised bewildered eyes
Up to the sun, as if above there were
An ear to hear my complaint,
A heart like mine
To take pity on the oppressed.

Who helped me
Against the Titans' arrogance?
Who rescued me from death,
From slavery?
Did not my holy and glowing heart,
Unaided, accomplish all?
And did it not, young and good,
Cheated, glow thankfulness
For its safety to him, to the sleeper above?

I pay homage to you? For what?
Have you ever relieved
The burdened man's anguish?
Have you ever assuaged
The frightened man's tears?
Was it not omnipotent Time
That forged me into manhood,
And eternal Fate,
My master's and yours?

Or did you think perhaps
That I should hate this life,
Flee into deserts
Because not all
The blossoms of dream grew ripe?

Here I sit, forming men
In my image,

A race to resemble me:
To suffer, to weep,
To enjoy, to be glad -
And never to heed you,
Like me!

In hindsight Goethe wrote[18] that his poem had "served as the kindling of an explosion which unveiled and brought to light the most secret relations of worthy persons: relations which, unknown to them, were slumbering in an otherwise highly enlightened society.... The rupture was so violent that on that occasion, through a series of occurrences, we lost one of our most worthy men, Mendelssohn." In Goethe's mind the unwanted publication of his poem by Jacobi initiated an almost mythical drama. For us at this point it is sufficient to note, with Goethe again, that it gave Lessing the occasion "to express himself in front of Jacobi on important points of thought and feeling."[19]

Lessing read Goethe's poem and gave it back to Jacobi, who not only had expected Lessing to be shocked by the poem, but also, more deeply, had hoped to find in Lessing a fellow opponent of Spinozism, who would help him criticize the world view implied in the poem. The conversation continued [85-86]:

Lessing: I take no offence; I long ago became acquainted with it first hand.

Jacobi: You know the poem?

Lessing: I have never read the poem; but I find it good.

Jacobi: I find it good too, in its way; otherwise I would not have shown it to you.

Lessing: That's not what I mean.... The point of view in which the poem is cast is my own point of view.... The

---

[18] *Dichtung und Wahrheit*, book 15 in *Goethes Werke*. München: Beck 1982[8], Vol. 10, p. 49 [written in 1813/1814].

[19] *Goethes Werke*, Vol. 10, p. 49.

orthodox concepts of the divinity are no longer for me; I cannot stand them. *Hen kai Pan!* I know naught else. This is also the tendency in this poem; and I must admit, I like it very much.

Jacobi: Then you would indeed be more or less in agreement with Spinoza.

Lessing: If I am to call myself by anybody's name, then I know none better.

Jacobi: Spinoza is good enough for me; but nevertheless there is scant benefit [schlechtes Heil] to be found in that name.

Lessing: Well fine, if that is what you think!... And yet... are you aware of a better one?

Here the conversation was interrupted. It resumed the next morning. Lessing wanted to talk about his *Hen kai Pan* because he had noticed the day before Jacobi's dismay at those words.

Jacobi: You surprised me and I probably turned from white to red for I felt confused. Dismay it was not. I certainly did not expect to find in you a Spinozist or pantheist. And you put it to me so bluntly. I had come chiefly in the hope of receiving your help against Spinoza.

Lessing: Then you really do know him?

Jacobi: I believe hardly anybody has known him as well as I.

Lessing: Then there is no help for you. Why don't you become his friend instead? There is no other philosophy but the philosophy of Spinoza.

The remaining part of the conversation was then devoted to answering Lessing's question: What did Jacobi hold to be the "spirit of Spinozism"? While Lessing inclined to think that such a spirit was to be found in the *Hen kai Pan*, "one and all," expression going back to Heraclitus [or to Xenophanes' *Hen to on kai Pan*] and appropriated by pantheism to denote the *one* God in the *whole* world, Jacobi's opinion was that Spinoza started out from the ancient principle *a nihilo nihil fit*, "nothing is made out of nothing," rejecting all forms of emanationism that would attempt to bridge the gap between the infinite and the finite; any attempt to derive the finite from the infinite amounted to the positing of something out of nothing. Since the passage from the infinite to the finite [creation] was impossible, Spinoza postulated one single immanent substance, an Infinite [Ensoph] immanent in the world; from it nothing emanated but it was posited as the eternal cause of the world with which it formed an indivisible unity.

Jacobi seemed eager to emphasize that Spinoza's pantheism was the inevitable result of his concept of infinity. Like G. Bruno and other philosophers of the 16th-17th centuries Spinoza was strongly impressed by the so-called "infinity of the world" and was thereby led to reject the idea of creation. If the cosmos was infinite, God was no longer transcendent; the Beyond was absorbed in the Here and the antithesis, God-nature, collapsed. For Spinoza the infinite substance was unique. It could not create, nor did it think since it was prior to thinking, and it had no individuality [102]. Thus God was equated with blind necessity on the one hand and with the world on the other.[20]

---

[20] A. Altmann, "Lessing und Jacobi: Das Gespräch über den Spinozismus", *LY* III, 1971, pp. 25-70 discusses and rejects Jacobi's opinion that Spinozism is connected with cabbala and that the cabbalistic "Ensoph" becomes in Spinoza the infinite substance [29-34]. See also his *Mendelssohn*, pp. 687-688.

Indeed Jacobi saw Spinozism as rationalized cabbala, an idea which he encountered in J.G. Wachter's works of 1699 and 1716: see Timm, *Gott und die Freiheit*, pp. 156-159. The possible connection between Spinoza's philosophy and cabbala is further explored by G. Scholem, "Die Wachtersche Kontroverse über den Spinozismus und ihre Folgen" in *Spinoza in der Frühzeit seiner religiösen Wirkung*, K. Gründer and W. Schmidt-Biggemann, eds., *WSA* XII, Heidelberg 1984, pp. 15-25; Scholem recalls that both Mendelssohn and Jacobi had read Wachter [25].

If one looks for mediation *à tout prix*, according to K. Hammacher, "Lessings Spinozismus..." in M. Vanhelleputte, ed., *Lessing und die Freiheit des Denkens*, *Tijdschrift voor de Studie van de Verlichting en van het Vrije Denken* 10[1982] 87-110, esp. 90-95, a form of "Christian cabbala" [represented by K. von Rosenroth, C.F. Meyer, etc.] was known to Lessing and would have led him to his Spinozist view of God in his late years.

χ   On the basis of his overall interpretation of the history of philosophy Jacobi was deeply convinced that pantheism constituted the only option for human reason left to its own devices. He therefore saw Spinoza as a "consequent rationalist";[21] strictly speaking, because it tries to explain everything, rationalism led to determinism, to fatalism, and finally to atheism.[22] In short "Spinozism is atheism," [123] said Jacobi in his compendium of assertions concerning Spinoza, thus summarizing one hundred years of anti-Spinoza polemics. It should be no surprise to see Jacobi hold a similar position against German idealism:[23] the latter merely unfolds the consequences of all philosophy and is thereby necessarily Spinozism. In the last analysis all metaphysical systems were atheistic for Jacobi because reason by itself can in no way warrant the assumption of an extra-worldly personal God. In order to circumvent this fateful destiny of all philosophizing or to overcome Spinoza, Jacobi found it naive to rely on speculative critique or on pure metaphysics; he knew of no other way out than a *salto mortale* that made one jump away from speculative knowledge into faith, hearkening no longer to the "head" but to the "heart."

Musings or not, such were Jacobi's views of the "spirit of Spinozism". Lessing's study of Spinoza, however sporadic, had led him to a view quite different from Jacobi's. At various places in Lessing's literary production we perceive clear echoes of Spinoza. This can be said already of "The Christianity of Reason" [1751/53]. Since his years in Breslau [1760-1765] he had intensified his reading of Spinoza and had come to the conclusion that Leibniz himself was a Spinozist at heart. He had discussed the issues of "God and the

---

[21] See Altmann, "Gespräch, pp. 28-40.

[22] "A-theist" and "deist" are quite the same for Jacobi; both are opposed to "theist"; both reject the idea of a personal God who would reveal himself; they recognize a cause of the world but this cause does not intervene once the world has come into existence. Because of this identification "a-theist" / "deist" Jacobi, when enumerating the themes of the first day conversation with Lessing [84] [first edition: "atheists, deists and Christians"], replaces "deists" by "theists" in the second edition, doubtless to avoid redundancy. I do not think, as does Hammacher in "Lessings Spinozismus...", p. 101, that "deists" in the first edition resulted from a typographical error.

[23] See Blumenberg, *Arbeit*, pp. 448-449.

world" with Mendelssohn[24] and expressed his views in a fragment, "On the Reality of Things Outside of God" [1763] published posthumously. Finally, traces of Spinoza can be found in *The Education of the Human Race* [1777-1780].We will come back later to those writings when dealing with Mendelssohn's interpretation of Lessing's Spinozism. For the moment, on the basis of Jacobi's report and keeping in mind those writings, it is not yet clear in what sense Lessing's position could be called pantheistic. Mendelssohn will call it "refined pantheism" and it seems that, for Lessing, God and the world represent two distinct stages[25] within the same reality in a way that reminds one of Plotinus. Quite certainly, *Hen kai Pan* or the unity of "natura naturans" and "natura naturata", God's transcendental unity, is not seen by Lessing as depriving God of reality or of thinking;[26] it does not amount to reducing God to thoughtlessness or to nothingness. Only: the world exists in God, by analogy with the Son's existing in God, as expressed in *The Education* § 73. It is precisely this idea of immanence that seems to be central to Lessing's understanding of Spinoza.

When Lessing said to Jacobi: "The orthodox concepts of the divinity are no longer for me," it is reasonable to assume that he meant "orthodox" in the style of S.J. Baumgarten's forensic theism;[27] he might have meant as well some neologist view à la Semler. At any rate he seems to dismiss the questionable representation of a God separated from the world which, he thinks, characterizes the traditional doctrine; he seems to reject all anthropomorphic thought that not only ascribes to God "our wretched way" of thinking [90], but also throws an unbridgeable gulf between us and a God "out there." Thus the *Hen kai Pan* embodies a protest against any separation between natural and supranatural. It does not include, though, a clear denial of their distinction. It would therefore be too rash, were one to read into the formula a denial not only that God is the cause of the world but also that he is distinct from it. As such, the formula does not

---

[24] Letter of April 17, 1763 in *Werke* VIII, pp. 719-720.

[25] Altmann, "Gespräch", p. 57 says "two aspects."

[26] See Altmann, "Gespräch", p. 57. Spinoza himself grants "cogitatio", but not "intellectus" to the infinite substance.

[27] See R. Schwarz, "Lessings 'Spinozismus'", *ZThK* 65 [1968] 271-290.

even deny the personal character of the deity. Rather, what is distinctive throughout Lessing's statements is his resolute tendency toward a theology of immanence and this-worldliness. This, of course, will have to be further substantiated.

The part of the conversations reported by Jacobi in the form of a dialogue ends as follows [96]:

Lessing: All in all I find your *salto mortale*[28] not bad and I can see how a man with a head on his shoulders might have to turn a somersault in order to get moving ahead. Take me with you if that is possible.

Jacobi: If you will just jump onto this springboard from which I am launched, that's all you need to do.

Lessing: Even to do that would entail a leap I may no longer ask of my old legs and my muddled head.

These are Lessing's last words in the conversation. Their irony cannot go unnoticed.[29]

---

[28] There is a certain analogy of situation between the change of order signified by Jacobi's *salto mortale* and the one referred to by Lessing with the image of the "ugly ditch" [in "On the Proof of the Spirit and of Power"]. On this imagery and its impact on 19th-20th century theology see G.E. Michalson, Jr., *Lessing's "Ugly Ditch": A Study of Theology and History*. University Park and London, 1985.

[29] S. Kierkegaard, *Concluding*, pp. 91-92, was able to feel their full irony and jest: "These 'last words' of Lessing, it will be remembered, gave occasion for quite a little scribbling at one time. The noble and enthusiastic Jacobi, who often speaks with amiable sympathy of the need of being understood by other thinkers, of how desirable it is to be in agreement with others, was the father confessor to whose lot it fell to preserve Lessing's last words. To be sure, it was no easy thing to essay the rôle of confessor for an ironical personality like Lessing, and Jacobi has had to suffer much: undeservedly, in so far as he has been unjustly criticized; deservedly, in so far as Lessing had by no means sent for him in the capacity of father confessor, still less requested him to make the conversation public, and least of all asked him to put the pathetic accent in the wrong place.

There is something extremely poetical in the entire situation: two such markedly developed personalities as Lessing and Jacobi in conversation with one another. The

The rest of Jacobi's report is a summary of diverse statements made by Lessing on different occasions. Essentially it boils down to Jacobi's brief formulation: "Lessing was adamant, insisting that everything be seen in terms of the natural;[30] I, for my part, asserted that there can be no natural philosophy of the supranatural and yet the two (the natural and the supranatural) are obviously givens." [97] Jacobi was inclined to equate Lessing's request with the rationalist urge to explain everything naturally, which he considered characteristic of Spinoza's rationalism.

Many other passages of the report would be worth mentioning for they reveal much about the two personalities: Jacobi's intense preoccupation with the course of European philosophy and his eagerness to warn people of its pitfalls; Lessing's own wit, his typical mixture of earnest and jest. The report also contains baffling passages that do not easily make sense and the scholarly well-trained Mendelssohn found it altogether muddled.

It is clear enough, however, that the centre of the conversations turned around the understanding of God and the question of the God-world relationship. It is significant that the main themes of philosophy of religion and of theodicy are touched upon in the conversations: God, freedom, immortality. They could hardly be avoided; once determinism is espoused [which is not to be equated with fatalism according to Lessing, who never tried to demonstrate that absence of identity, however], a theodicy is

---

inexhaustible spokesman for enthusiasm as observer, and the subtle Lessing as catechumen. Jacobi takes it upon himself to examine Lessing, to find out how things really stand with him. What happens? To his horror he discovers that Lessing is at bottom a Spinozist. The enthusiastic Jacobi ventures upon extreme measures, and proposes to him the only saving *salto mortale*."

[30] Because of his doctrine of natural necessity and determinism, Lessing seems to have consequently transferred to the theological scene the prescription he had expressed in the *Hamburger Dramaturgie* [1769] concerning the stage: "However convinced we might be of the direct actions of grace, they can please us very little on the stage where everything that belongs to the character of the persons must result from the most natural causes. Only in the physical world do we tolerate miracles; in the moral world everything must keep its orderly course." *Werke* IV, p. 239. See also Lessing's statements on the "natural course of things" in *Werke* VII, pp. 283 and 301

needed. On those topics Jacobi had received the definite impression that "at the end of his life Lessing was a firm Spinozist." We must now try to bring out the extent to which Jacobi's report is to affect our understanding of Lessing's relationship to the philosophy of Spinoza.

2. The Reliability of Jacobi's Report

The authenticity of Jacobi's account has never been questioned. Contemporaries of Jacobi as well as recent scholars all recognize that the report is trustworthy.[31] Elise Reimarus found the rendering of the conversations lively, likely, and reliable, "as though one would hear them both talk, with all the mental sharpness and characteristic humour." Herder agreed: "Lessing is so presented that I can see and hear him speak." Mendelssohn himself never went so far as to doubt that the report was referring to events that had really taken place.

At two points, however, in Jacobi's account there is something that does not quite fit.[32] First, how could the conversation pass directly from the reading of Goethe's poem "Prometheus" to a discussion of Spinoza? I shall come back later to the interpretation of the poem. For his part, Scholz finds the poem "totally un-Spinozist"[33] and draws attention to the opposition "between the roots of the Promethean rebellion and the motives of Spinoza's *Gelassenheit*"[34]; instead he sees in it a virulent critique of the supranaturalistic faith in providence and his question becomes: How does one pass from a denial of providence to an affirmation of pantheism? In 1785 Jacobi himself seems to have interpreted the poem as a critique of providence[35] while Mendelssohn could not understand "the pleasure found in bad verse, most unnatural in a

---

[31] See Scholz, *Hauptschriften*, p. lxiii; *Werke*, VIII, p. 749.

[32] See Scholz, *Hauptschriften*, pp. lxiii-lxvii; *Werke*, VIII, p. 749.

[33] Scholz, *Hauptschriften*, p. lxiii; see p. lxxxii [Nicolai].

[34] Scholz, *Hauptschriften*, p. lxv.

[35] In Scholz, *Hauptschriften*, p.12* [note 30 to p. 304]: "This poem directed against all providence...."

Lessing.... Thou wretched judge of art! how low must you have fallen, that you find this paltry thing in earnest good!" [133, 136][36]

But was the poem so totally unrelated to the spirit of Spinoza? Blumenberg[37] thinks he can detect here a possible, if not compelling connection, provided one pays attention to the "basic mood of the ancient tragedy" embodied in the poem. "For the ultimate common element between polytheism and pantheism, Epicureanism and Spinozism has always been seen in the rejection of the divine concern for man." Clearly, however, the connection with Spinoza offered by the poem remains a loose one. It is first established in the conversation by Jacobi himself who thus puts the alleged Spinozism of the poem so to speak in the mouth of Lessing[38] and artificially leads him to a confession of sorts.[39] I will come back to the interpretation of the poem below and will also look at what Lessing himself saw in it.

A second "inconsistency" in Jacobi's account has to do with the ② statement: "[Lessing] believed that a continuation of man's personal life after death was not unlikely." [98] This formulation clashes too directly with the last paragraphs of *The Education* [especially §§ 94-100] for one not to think that here Jacobi has misunderstood something.

---

[36] Altogether, Mendelssohn was puzzled by the whole conversation. "... I fail totally to discern the stamp of Lessing's character in anything he contributes; I miss his acumen, I miss his humour, I miss his philosophy, and I miss his critical sense." [133] But it is only in the irritated mood of *An die Freunde Lessings* that Mendelssohn will question the very meaning Jacobi's report gave to Lessing's words.

[37] Blumenberg, *Arbeit*, p. 457.

[38] See Scholz, *Hauptschriften*, p. lxv, note 3: "... the name of Spinoza is first pronounced by Jacobi. This seems to me to indicate that the combination 'Prometheus-Spinoza' is to be attributed exclusively to Jacobi and may not be traced back to Lessing."

[39] In his reconstruction of the intellectual atmosphere around 1780 H. Timm, *Gott und die Freiheit*, p. 190 argues that the connection Prometheus-Spinoza remains unclear only to those who have not understood the link between the *Sturm und Drang* of the 1770s, represented by Prometheus, and the religious Spinozism of the 1780s. I do not question the validity of Timm's view, but I still believe that such "clear connection" is far from being immediate and appears only as the result of a strained search for mediation and at the cost of postulated associations. The mere logical possibility of a connection, Prometheus-Spinoza, is no proof of its actuality.

Once these two reservations have been mentioned, we are left with a report that is, on the whole, credible. And in it Lessing sides with Spinoza in a way that could be called a confession. Why did Lessing side with Spinoza? How are we to understand his "confession"?

3. Lessing's "Character"

In many respects Jacobi's account must fall short of the lively zest of the conversations that took place in July and August 1780. Furthermore, it would be wrong to expect Jacobi to show total empathy with Lessing: after all, this was their first personal encounter. Thus it should not be a cause for surprise if we notice that Jacobi tends to take Lessing's words literally and to interpret them "dogmatically". Lessing's friends, who esteemed him for his prodigious mixture of jest and earnest, were, for the most part, inclined to interpret the dialogue as one more typical exercise in thought[40] in which Lessing's real position is revealed only indirectly and, at that, only by bringing to it real familiarity with the man and much skill at deciphering.

It is important at this point to recall, as did his friends, how Lessing would behave in a "serious" conversation. We have many witnesses as to his habit of siding with the weaker party. This characteristic feature is relevant to an interpretation of his conversations with Jacobi, since Jacobi, right at the outset, adopts

---

[40] I am referring here to the distinction made by Lessing in a letter to his brother [letter of March 16, 1778 in *Werke* VIII, p. 608]: "... I must adjust my weapons depending on my opponent, and I would not write *dogmatikos* [= with absolute claim at validity] everything that I write *gymnastikos* [= by way of exercise]."

The couple *dogmatikos-gymnastikos* goes back to Origen, *On the First Principles*, Pref. 3, as worded by Athanasius.

See also the illuminating statement made by Lessing in 1776 [*Werke* VIII, p. 549], which should be kept in mind when interpreting some of the amazing assertions Lessing made to Jacobi: "It is mere pity that I cannot think without a pen in my hand! yes, it is! I only think for my own instruction. If my thoughts please me in the end, I tear the paper to pieces. If they do not please me, I publish them. If somebody teaches me better, I am happy to take a little humiliation."

an anti-Spinozist position which, in the eyes of Lessing, not only puts Spinoza under attack but also tends to make the now silent Spinoza appear defenceless. Hence the emphatic statement by Lessing: "There is no other philosophy but the philosophy of Spinoza.... If I am to call myself by anybody's name, then I know none better ." [85, 86]

Here are some instances of Lessing's taking, "for the sake of exercise", a position that is opposite that of his partner in dialogue, and playing the devil's advocate. C.F. Nicolai recalls that Lessing, in a debate, had "the skill either to take the weaker side or, if somebody presented the *pro*, to hunt right away for the *contra* with rare sharpness."[41] During the Seven-Year War which saw Prussia and Saxony in opposite camps, the same Nicolai reports that Lessing, "as long as he was in Leipzig would in society take the party of Prussia and in Berlin, that of Saxony."[42] It was his habit to side with the weaker.[43] Much of his literary activity was determined by this habit. Beginning with his play *Die Juden* [1749] and the essay *Gedanken über die Herrnhuter* [1750] right down to his Wolfenbüttel writings, his publications show a continuous interest for "Rettungen" [rescues] in which Lessing attempts to "save" some deviant, individual or collective, from the condemning judgment of the masses or of tradition.

Thus Lessing's friends were not surprised to hear that in his conversations with Jacobi he had defended Spinoza. Lessing "could not easily suffer the all-too-decisive attitude and he often liked to take the side which was the weaker or the reverse of what somebody would affirm peremptorily."[44] In such circumstances one was well advised "not to regard everything he said as a confession of faith."[45] Mendelssohn knew that Lessing "was able to defend even an error with zeal ... when the reasons invoked for its refutation were not sufficient." [73] He also knew that Lessing was at his best when irritated, and that he was irritated by poor arguments.

---

[41] In Daunicht, *Lessing*, p. 72.

[42] In Daunicht, *Lessing*, p. 150; see also pp. 151, 216-217.

[43] See Daunicht, *Lessing*, pp. 197, 281.

[44] Nicolai in Daunicht, *Lessing*, p. 587.

[45] C.T. Weiße in Daunicht, *Lessing*, p. 586.

Lessing's brother shared the same general opinion. "He wanted to come to the aid of the oppressed more than to celebrate triumph with the victorious."[46] That is why, "against Jacobi who seized the spirit of Spinoza which he could just not follow, Lessing was candid, for fun and in earnest, sometimes a blind pantheist, sometimes a refined one."[47] Those who knew Lessing well were inclined to smile at Jacobi's dogmatic seriousness about a conversation he had had with a highly sophisticated man he met for the first time. As Nicolai recalled, familiarity with Lessing had brought to his German friends something they so seldom encountered otherwise: "In society he was indeed a lover of something which the English people call fun and for which our solemn German countrymen have no word and perhaps even only seldom any sense at all...."[48]

It is on this last trait of Lessing's character that other friends based their spiteful interpretation of the Spinoza conversations. They thought that Lessing had had a good time at Jacobi's expense. This view is not easily reconcilable with the undeniable respect Lessing elsewhere showed for Jacobi. At any rate the opinion that Lessing had taken Jacobi for a ride was held by some. A.G. Kästner wrote to Nicolai in 1786: "One should really tell Herr Jacobi in black and white that Lessing had the best of him. Everybody who has known Lessing will confirm that."[49] Even the old Gleim lost his

---

[46] K.G. Lessing in Daunicht, *Lessing*, p. 592.

[47] In Daunicht, *Lessing*, p. 590.

[48] In Daunicht, *Lessing*, p. 587.

[49] In Daunicht, *Lessing*, p. 586. Immediately after the publication of Jacobi's Spinoza book some among the persons closest to Lessing had already expressed similar views. See for instance Elise's letter to Mendelssohn, October 18, 1785 in M. Mendelssohn, *Gesammelte Schriften*, Vol. 13, pp. 315, where she declares herself to be appalled at Jacobi's divulgence of "the minute irrelevant details of a private conversation, indeed of a confidential private joke of our deceased friend." See also K.G. Lessing's letter to Mendelssohn, October 19, 1785 [pp. 318-319]: "Don't you think that my brother was having a joke with Jacobi? In part he wanted to sound him out to see whether he had read Spinoza at all and to what extent he had understood him or not; further, many passages show most clearly that he was poking fun at him. For him it was both inclination and cunning to pretend the contrary of that which the other seemed to be so full of; thereby he did not precisely intend to make the other into an -ist, but only

usual serenity on this issue: "What for God's sake drove the dear man [Jacobi] to broadcast to the whole world through gossiping that Lessing would have become an atheist?... How could the dear man be so blind as not to see that Lessing had the best of him with his Spinoza, especially with the so much praised Prometheus poem in which after all there is absolutely nothing so sublime."[50]

It is significant that Mendelssohn did not think he had to go along without qualification with similar trivializing of Lessing's reported statements. Apparently he saw no point in trying to exonerate Lessing from any allegiance to Spinoza. Rather he conceded that his friend admitted to an inclination toward pantheism, even toward pantheism in the form Spinoza had given it. This aspect of Jacobi's "revelation" had nothing to upset Mendelssohn, at least so he claimed. Referring to Lessing's early fragment "The Christianity of Reason," Mendelssohn could write: "I had already been aware that in his earliest youth our friend had inclined to pantheism.... The news that Lessing was a Spinozist could in consequence neither astonish nor alienate me." [130]

Mendelssohn's outward composure, however, could not totally hide his anger or his helplessness in regard to Jacobi's disclosure. Two points, in particular, in Jacobi's account had sparked his growing irritation. The first one had deeply wounded him; it was Jacobi's innuendo that Lessing, in spite of their lifelong friendship, had not judged him strong enough to hear his real thoughts [132, 134]. The second irritating point was Jacobi's identification of Spinozism with atheism, which amounted to a slandering of Lessing's reputation.

On the first point Mendelssohn could not do better than to parade the attitude of one who had known all along of Lessing's

---

to explore the measure of his critical sense." Lessing's brother wrote similar things again to Mendelssohn on October 24, 1785 [p. 322].

[50] J.W.L Gleim in Daunicht, *Lessing*, p. 585. Such an outburst is indeed surprising on the part of Gleim. On November 21, 1781 [in F.H. Jacobi, *Briefwechsel* I,2. Ed. by M. Brüggen and W. Sudhof. Stuttgart/Bad Cannstadt 1981, pp. 378-380] he had criticized Goethe for doing the very same thing [only worse, as I will recall below] he now attributes to Lessing. He had written to an humiliated Jacobi: "Goethe makes fun of his friends.... This is the reason, I think, why Lessing never became his friend."

Spinozist leanings. - How then to account for the at times jocular, at times extreme words of Lessing reported by Jacobi? Mendelssohn did not question the authenticity of Jacobi's report but he did passionately doubt that Lessing had intended to entrust Jacobi with a special secret and to make him a genuine confidence [133-36]; against the view that those conversations could rightly be taken for an authentic unveiling of the heart on the part of Lessing, Mendelssohn went as far as to suggest that there was a kind of simulation in Lessing's attitude [136]. To top it off, Mendelssohn claimed to see through Jacobi's goal in publishing his Spinoza book: to make an example of Lessing [136], to use Lessing in order to deter people from speculation and bring them back to faith [134-136]. Jacobi, Mendelssohn claimed, made Lessing speak on his behalf and for his own cause.

Replying to the second point, Mendelssohn got ahead of Jacobi's publication of his account, distinguishing in his *Morgenstunden* two forms of pantheism and attributing to Lessing only what he called "refined pantheism," thus defusing in advance the impact of Jacobi's revelation.

4. Spinozism and Goethe's Poem

Before elaborating on the issues just mentioned, I wish to note some puzzling elements in Jacobi's account of his conversations with Lessing. Two misunderstandings on Jacobi's part appear at the beginning of his account and reveal a peculiar eagerness to give the conversation a certain direction. One misunderstanding seems at first sight to be without significance; it occurs when Lessing, after reading Goethe's poem, says: "I have been familiar with it for a long time." Jacobi mistakenly understands that Lessing already knew the poem or had read it. Lessing corrects him on this.

The second misunderstanding will determine the course of the remaining conversation. It occurs after Lessing said that he meant not the poem itself but its point of view. Then Jacobi rushes to declare, and Lessing does not object this time, that the point of view of the poem is taken from Spinoza; he might have been thinking of the lines of the poem alluding to blind necessity ["omnipotent Time", "eternal Fate"]. Says Altmann: "The god of gods, before whom Jupiter bows his head, is 'all powerful Time and eternal Fate, my lord and thine,' the *moira* of the Greeks, or in Spinoza's terms [as understood by Jacobi], the one, eternal substance prior to all intellect and will."[51] The Spinozist point of view of the poem was so evident to Jacobi[52] that he did not hesitate, as it were, to put Spinoza in Lessing's mouth. After all, he had come to receive from Lessing his "help against Spinoza" [86]; it had to be expected, should the conversation come to the topic of Spinoza, that Jacobi would be the one to mention his name first.

What then could Lessing have meant when he said on July 6: "I long ago became acquainted with it first hand"? [85] In answer to this question two clues are available to us. The first one comes from Jacobi himself in reference to a later conversation with Lessing [August 15, 1780] and suggests that Lessing had not thought of Spinoza at this point in the July dialogue: "Still on the morning of our separation in Halberstadt at breakfast... Lessing requested again from me the 'Prometheus' and again praised and admired in it the authentic living spirit of Antiquity, according to form and content."[53] This story should make clear that Lessing did not have Spinoza in mind when he read Goethe's poem, but rather the point of view of the ancient tragedy of Aeschylus.[54] The poem pleased Lessing not because of its postulated Spinozism, but because

---

[51] A. Altmann, *Mendelssohn*, p. 619. See also his "Gespräch, pp. 34-35.

[52] To Mendelssohn as well at first; see his initial reaction in the letter of November 18, 1783 to Elise R. [in *Gesammelte Schriften*, Vol. 13, p. 158]: "The so-called Spinozist system cannot be presented in a more felicitous manner in all its nakedness" than in this poem. Two years later, though, Mendelssohn will call the poem "this paltry thing", made of "bad verse." [85, 89]

[53] In Scholz, *Hauptschriften*, p. lxv, note 3; pp. 12*-13* [note 31 to page 304]; Daunicht, *Lessing*, p. 531; see also Blumenberg, *Arbeit*, p. 457.

[54] To Hamann, who mentioned Aeschylus as representing here the spirit of Antiquity praised by Lessing, Jacobi replied that the two dialogues of Lucian seemed to him to be closer to the Prometheus poem than the tragedy of Aeschylus. Hamann, *Briefwechsel*. Wiesbaden 1955 ff., Vol. V, pp. 271, 301 [quoted by Altmann, "Gespräch", pp. 43 and 68]. See also Jacobi in Scholz, *Hauptschriften*, pp. 76-77 note, where a reference to Lucian was already found.

of its affinity with the spirit of Antiquity.[55] What was then the point of view of Antiquity which had found its dramatic expression in the saga of *Prometheus Bound*? This leads us to the second clue available for decoding Lessing's puzzling statement.

The second clue is provided directly by Lessing himself and is found in Jacobi's report immediately following Lessing's statement, "The orthodox concepts of the divinity are no longer for me." [85] He preferred the ancient concepts of polytheism or those of Epicureanism to the traditional Judaeo-Christian concepts of the divinity as he had come to know them. It seems that for Lessing the orthodox ideas of God embodied a view of transcendence that he found repressive; he preferred either the indifference of the Epicurean gods or the indignation of Prometheus. There he found a better account of humanity's sense of having come of age,[56] of the genius' creative autonomy, and of the fact that we are called upon to live "as though there would be no God." [Grotius] At any rate, a theology of immanence that represents the gods either as involved in human affairs or as urging men to responsibility, appeared to Lessing more satisfying than contemporary theological views of God's despotic will and of his total separation from the world. Now while the principle of immanence as such does not lead to atheism,[57] it certainly calls for a new interpretation of the divine and a less anthropomorphic view of God.

It appears that Lessing's spontaneous preference for a theology of immanence, vaguely hinted at in the Prometheus poem, led him to condone Jacobi's introduction of Spinoza's name into the conversation.[58] After all, the idea of immanence is essential to

---

[55] Beside the paganism of the Prometheus poem, its mood might have been attractive to Lessing and this, for personal reasons: he liked the mood of rebellion of the poem; after the death of one's son and wife, who would not be tempted by rebellion?

[56] On this point see Altmann, "Gespräch", pp. 43-44.

[57] See Scholz, *Hauptschriften*, p. lxvi.

[58] Timm, *Gott und die Freiheit*, pp. 159-184, 190-197, 200-208 goes through a painstaking inventory in order to make the identification Spinoza-Prometheus likely or natural. Timm's analysis remains abstract, however, based on assumed associations and a commentary that sets itself the agenda of filling all the gaps encountered in the "conversations," of explaining everything seriously, even the jokes. For my part, I

Spinoza's system. It is obviously not foreign to philosophy either. It is even essential to the philosophical enterprise as such. And because Spinoza built his philosophy exclusively upon the principle of immanence, there is ground for saying that his is the best philosophy. "There is no other philosophy but the philosophy of Spinoza."

Now, if the link between the Prometheus poem and the spirit of Spinoza was not quite obvious to Lessing [although he accepted it when proposed by Jacobi], how can we explain that such a connection seems to have been evident to Jacobi? My contention is that the poem is not intrinsically Spinozist [for instance, it juxtaposes without "mediation" the clashing views of rebellion and submission: rebellion against Zeus and the gods, and submission to Fate and Time, the real God; the critique of providence found in the poem is not identical with a pantheistic confession: all problems created, it could be said, by any attempt at a philosophical reading of a poetical work]; it only became Spinozist for Jacobi due to the circumstances of his difficult friendship with Goethe.

When Jacobi and Goethe met for the first time in the Summer of 1774, two incidents took place: first, Goethe told Jacobi about his being busy with the figure of Prometheus and then [or soon after] gave him his Prometheus poem to read; second, in lengthy and fiery conversations, Goethe made clear that he was infatuated with Spinoza. Those two incidents became linked together in Jacobi's mind and their union prepared for his attribution of the Prometheus work to the spirit of Spinoza. When, six years later, Jacobi's friendship with Goethe not only had cooled off, but also had been scoffed at [remember the parody of Ettersburg when Goethe "crucified" Jacobi's *Woldemar*, nailed it to a tree and made fun of it before his companions], Jacobi appeared at a loss to grasp the roots of Goethe's behaviour. Trying to understand what kind of individual Goethe was, Jacobi certainly relived the scene of their first encounter when he had heard Goethe's confidences concerning both his reading of Spinoza and his work on Prometheus. The wounded friend now travelled with Goethe's poem in his luggage. He knew that the author of that poem was the same person who

---

believe that the fragmentary character of the report should be respected as well as the logical leaps in the conversations themselves.

had been infatuated with Spinoza. That is why, in front of Lessing, Jacobi had no hesitation in interpreting the Prometheus poem as Spinozist: not for intrinsic reasons, for such an interpretation was anything but compelling, but for extrinsic ones. Jacobi had for some time already combined Goethe's enthusiasm for Spinoza with the revolutionary posture depicted in the poem. By virtue of such an association he could hear the spirit of Spinoza speak through the poem.

What then was Spinozist in the Prometheus poem? Very little for Lessing. Not much more for Jacobi. In itself the poem embodied Goethe's wrestling with the enormous pressure under which the twenty-five years old poet found himself, "fesselt" like Prometheus, bound by professional worries and social relations; Goethe had recourse to the symbol of Prometheus in an effort to clarify his situation of a creative genius in the midst of numerous invitations to yield to surrounding pressures. If Jacobi had been able to connect Prometheus and Spinoza, it was because he knew that Goethe, at the same time as he was coming to terms with his own situation with the help of the Prometheus myth, was also reading Spinoza with the enthusiasm of one who has found his real father and saviour. Thus, for Jacobi, Prometheus and Spinoza became associated and their voices fused. On the basis of this association Jacobi could declare to Lessing straight out: If you like this poem, then you also like Spinoza. And Lessing did not object to the introduction of the name of Spinoza at this point.

Thus began the "Spinoza conversations" between Lessing and Jacobi. In them it soon became clear, as already indicated, that two diverging views of Spinozism faced one another, Jacobi's and Lessing's, although Jacobi's report assumes a basic agreement. A. Altmann has tested this assumed agreement and convincingly shown that we have here two distinct conceptions of Spinozism.[59] Jacobi does not make any distinction between a full-fledged pantheism that ultimately divinizes the world through blending the finite with the infinite [pantheism which Jacobi means every time he says "Spinoza" or "Spinozism"], and a form of pantheism that maintains the existence of the finite *within* the infinite, pantheism which Mendelssohn wished to call "refined pantheism" and which might be

---

[59] Altmann, "Gespräch", pp. 25-58.

better called "panentheism", meaning that everything exists in some way *in* God.

Only implicit in the conversations, such a distinction must be made explicit, and this on historical grounds: for in the course of the "pantheism debate" the distinction did give birth to two fronts and two schools of interpretation of Lessing-the-Spinozist [or pantheist], mainly represented by Jacobi and Mendelssohn respectively. The question as to whether or not the distinction is objectively grounded must remain open at this point. What concerns me is the fact that it was made. Thus the conversation between Jacobi and Lessing on the theme of Spinoza, with its double view of Spinozism, brought about the question of Lessing's Spinozism and was prolonged by the pantheism debate between Jacobi and Mendelssohn. We now turn to this debate in order to gain a better understanding of the two opposing interpretations of Lessing's thought.

5. Jacobi and Lessing's Spinozism

In two works Jacobi presented at length his conception of Spinoza and applied it to the thought of Lessing in an effort to show him as a consequent Spinozist: *Über die Lehre des Spinoza in Briefen an den Herrn Moses Mendelssohn*,[60] which contains the correspondence with Mendelssohn, including the report of his conversations with Lessing, and *Wider Mendelssohns Beschuldigungen in dessen Schreiben an die Freunde Lessings*.[61] The first writing is the more informative with its lengthy dissertations on Spinozism in the form of letters and, in the second edition, in the form of *Beylagen* [Annexes];[62] from it we can grasp what Jacobi understood the "spirit of Spinozism" to be.

---

[60] Breslau 1785[1], 1789[2], Leipzig 1819 in *Werke* IV, 1-2. Reproduced by Scholz, *Hauptschriften*, pp. 45-282.

[61] Leipzig 1786[1], 1819 in *Werke* IV, 2. Reproduced by Scholz, *Hauptschriften*, pp. 327-364 [without the first part].

[62] The *Beylagen* are made of essays, explanations, and discussions by Jacobi; they deal with various aspects of pantheism and contain an especially relevant excerpt from G. Bruno.

X   For him Spinozism is, "according to its form, the system of consequent rationalism";[63] according to its content, it is consequent atheism.[64] How does it evolve? Left to its own devices, reason inevitably ends up in pantheism; pure reason can only conceive of an immanent infinite which is *Hen kai Pan*, and cannot present any grounds for admitting a personal God distinct from the world.[65] Why is such rationalism ultimately atheistic? On this point Jacobi had an original contribution to make;[66] he was able to show with forceful arguments how, strictly speaking, Spinozist atheism flows from Spinozist rationalism: to identify God with the blind necessity of nature is to eliminate God as a distinct personal being and to espouse deism, which is the same as atheism for Jacobi. From this view the personalist Jacobi derives a more general conclusion: all metaphysical systems, because they rest upon reason alone, are at bottom atheistic; thus for Jacobi the philosophical enterprise as such is doomed.[67] Those who, dissatisfied with traditional supranaturalist theism, take refuge in pantheism and invoke its appeal to fill human consciousness with a new religious pathos, as was done increasingly around Jacobi, must be told of the fatal risk

---

[63] As formulated by Scholz, *Hauptschriften*, p. xix.

[64] It is about Spinozism that Jacobi says this. As for Spinoza himself the picture should be different. The accusation of atheism, universally thrown at Spinoza between 1670 and 1790, evokes the similar accusation made against Christianity in its beginnings and reported by Justin Martyr when he writes: "Hence we are called atheists. And we confess that we are atheists, so far as gods of this sort [Graeco-Roman] are concerned, but not with respect to the most true God...." [*I Apology* 6] Up to Spinoza, philosophy used to infer God from the world and to devise proofs for his existence through a kind of induction, thus concluding from the world to God. That approach was indeed subverted by Spinoza. In a sense he could have paraphrased Justin: "Yes, we are atheists of all those proofs...." As in the case of Justin this statement should obviously not be taken for a confession of atheism *simpliciter*. Rather, God's existence is so absolutely certain for Spinoza that he is naturally inclined to let God occupy the whole place and must then wrestle with the problem of conceiving anything beside God.

[65] See Altmann, "Gespräch", pp. 32-33.

[66] See Scholz, *Hauptschriften*, p. xxi.

[67] This is the way Mendelssohn understood Jacobi's stance on the fateful destiny of speculative reason. "Jacobi... tries to convince me that speculative reason, when consistent, leads perforce to Spinozism; he tried to persuade me that, once someone has reached the precipitous peaks of Metaphysics, there is no recourse but to turn one's back on all philosophy and plunge head first into the depths of faith." [140]

they run: they all end up embracing Spinoza. The warning is given first of all to Herder and Goethe;[68] it is further given to nascent German idealism which, in the eyes of Jacobi, embodies the fundamental concern of all philosophy[69] and is thereby necessarily Spinozist. Therefore there is a sense in which Jacobi could have said with Lessing: "There is no other philosophy but the philosophy of Spinoza." But Jacobi does not rest content with pointing to the ✗ thrust of all philosophizing and its dilemma; he seeks a way out of it and uses Spinoza as a springboard for his *salto mortale* into the immediacy of a faith based on feeling.

When Jacobi declared that "Lessing was in his final days a firm ✗ Spinozist," the statement, now detailed in his account of the conversations, carried the ominous weight of Jacobi's interpretation of Spinoza. The declaration certainly had an explosive charge and Lessing's friends understood only too well what it implied. They were well aware of the fundamental critique and of the denunciation to which the statement amounted. It was suggested that rational theism had been for Lessing a mere "exoteric cover" for his Spinozism.[70] And to reveal Lessing as a Spinozist was identical for Jacobi with making him an atheist.[71] The friends reacted vehemently. Had not Jacobi set a trap for Lessing and, as it were, pushed him to confess an allegiance to Spinoza? [see 133] Could Lessing have meant it? Had he not said what he said only "for the sake of exercise"? How was Lessing's behaviour to be understood?

In addition to the denunciation of Lessing as a secret atheist, what upset his friends perhaps still more were the circumstances of Jacobi's revelation. Elise Reimarus, an otherwise close friend of Jacobi, accused him of plain indiscretion for broadcasting, beyond the circle of intimate friends, "the whole detail of a confidential conversation, of those little jokes which one ventures only with the confidants of one's soul and head and which are transformed into

---

[68] See Timm, *Gott und die Freiheit*, esp. pp. 315-320.

[69] See Blumenberg, *Arbeit*, p. 448.

[70] See Scholz, *Hauptschriften*, p. lix.

[71] It also amounted to making the leading philosophers of Prussia and all the pseudo-Christian neo-Spinozists of his time suspect of atheism. See Timm, *Gott und die Freiheit*, p. 31.

blasphemies as soon as they are repeated outside that narrow circle."[72] She was appalled at the idea of seeing Lessing's private thoughts handed over to the mob, to a public unable to discern. "I might have been led by prejudice, but I was shocked as I saw our Lessing thus exposed before a world that does not understand him, that cannot judge him, that is not worthy of seeing him without a veil."[73]

Mendelssohn felt the same way. "A friend entrusts a confession to his ears, and he betrays it to the public; a friend, as his life is drawing to a close, makes him the confidant of his frailty, and this he uses to stain the man's memory for all posterity." [133] In the whole affair Mendelssohn was certainly not blameless; he had awkwardly hidden the manuscript of his *Morgenstunden* from Jacobi while showing it to other friends and had misled Jacobi into thinking that he was to make public use of the content of their correspondence. Nevertheless he felt personally hurt by Jacobi's manners: Jacobi had now published his own letters without his permission and, still worse, he would have the readers believe that Lessing had concealed from him such important things as his heartfelt philosophical position. "I must confess, it would humble me greatly, had our friend Lessing deemed me... to be unworthy of the confidence that another mortal was able to gain on such short acquaintance, and this after I had lived with him in intimate friendship for over thirty years...." [132][74]

---

[72] Letter of October 24, 1785 to Jacobi in Scholz, *Hauptschriften*, pp. lxxxvi-lxxxvii. See also her letter of October 18, 1785 to Mendelssohn: "... Just looking at the title [*Über die Lehre des Spinoza in Briefen an den Herrn Moses Mendelssohn*] already made my heart skip a beat; but it got worse when, in the writing itself, I saw exposed to the eyes of the mocking or afflicted public not only all the minute and therefore irrelevant details of a private correspondence, but also all the minute and therefore irrelevant details of a private conversation, indeed of a confidential private joke of our deceased friend." In M. Mendelssohn, *Gesammelte Schriften*. Vol. 13, p. 315.

[73] In Scholz, *Hauptschriften*, p. lxxxvi.

[74] These two main motives of Mendelssohn's vexation are mentioned side by side in a letter to I. Kant of October 16, 1785 [quoted by Altmann, *Mendelssohn*, p. 705]: "With what right one permits oneself nowadays... the publication of a private correspondence without having asked for and obtained permission from the correspondents is incomprehensible to me. Moreover: Lessing is alleged to have confessed to him, i.e., to

At this point it becomes imperative to try to gain more clarity as to the two events initiated by Jacobi: What was his interest in meeting with Lessing in the first place? What was his intention in publishing the details of their conversations?

A/ For some time already Jacobi had been eager to meet with Lessing. He knew of his writings. He admired him; although some of his writings could hardly meet with his approval, especially some passages of *The Education of the Human Race* [§§ 33, 73, 78...]. But it quite doubtful that Jacobi intended to discuss precisely § 73 with Lessing:[75] that would be to look, in hindsight, for a point of contact with Spinozism in Lessing himself; the report of the conversations reveals nothing of such an intention. The report says rather that Jacobi came to Lessing with Goethe's poem in his luggage. There is no reason to doubt Jacobi's clear words: he had come to Lessing in order to get assistance from him against Spinoza whose ghost he perceived in Goethe's poem. Now, in front of Lessing, the tables are turned and Jacobi must show Lessing in

---

Jacobi, that he had never revealed his true philosophical principles to me, his intimate philosophical friend of thirty years' standing."

[75] That Jacobi proposed to talk about § 73 of *The Education* is postulated by P. Rilla [editor of G.E. Lessing, *Gesammelte Werke*. Vol. IX. Berlin/Weimar 1954-1958, p. 862 n. 1] but is generally rejected, e.g., by Blumenberg, *Arbeit*, p. 446. We recall that § 73 deals with an attempt at speculatively justifying the doctrine of the Trinity or, conversely, at deriving the transcendental *Hen kai Pan* from the trinitarian conception of God's self-consciousness. Until very recently it was usually said that Jacobi's letter to Lessing, proposing themes for conversation, was lost. Now the new edition of Jacobi's correspondence, *Briefwechsel* I.2, pp. 141-142 contains a letter, dated June 1, 1780, which could well be the one whose disappearance was assumed. In it, after mentioning that he has read *The Education* with pleasure, Jacobi does propose themes for discussion: including a fragment he published in *Merkur* [the fragment is a continuation of *Woldemar*], he asks Lessing to read the second part about which he would like to talk with him; he would be pleased if Lessing would also look at his fourth letter [published in 1774] on Pauw's *Recherches sur les Egyptiens et les Chinois*. But it is correct: no mention is made of § 73 of *The Education*.

what he thinks the spirit of Spinoza consists and what the problem with it is.[76]

Thus Jacobi feels entrusted with the task of teaching Lessing about Spinoza.[77] The report witnesses to Jacobi's self-confidence and even brio in performing his task; Mendelssohn will remark that, curiously, "all reasonable arguments are attributed to Herr Jacobi.... Lessing offers not even one significant counter-proposition.... Could Lessing, in a sincere, intimate outpouring of the heart, forget himself to such a degree?" [133] Moreover, Jacobi speaks with a sense of mission. He is convinced that the rationalism creeping into German philosophy is ill-fated; rational theism is right in line with Spinoza and more often than not serves as a mere cover for Spinozism: in fact, it leads to atheism. To Jacobi's taste, Lessing flirts a little too much with the dormant dragon and he must be warned of its destructive powers.

Obviously, Jacobi was greatly fascinated by Spinoza, as he was by rational thinking itself. He was fascinated to the point that, when explaining Spinoza to Mendelssohn, the latter at times thought he was confronted with a champion of Spinozism and even considered, for a while, having "him [Jacobi] speak in Spinoza's stead" when writing his *Morgenstunden* [117]. Likewise, one reason why Jacobi decided to go ahead with his publication of *Über die Lehre des Spinoza* was that he feared Mendelssohn, in his

---

[76] On Lessing's attitude at this turn of the conversation, see Altmann, *Mendelssohn*, p. 621: "Lessing noticed at the outset Jacobi's opposition to Spinozism as a viable philosophy, and it would have been entirely consistent with his character to have posed as a Spinozist. The jocularity of some of Lessing's remarks, especially his 'cabbalistic' references to himself as divinity in the state of 'contraction', which were quoted in this context, would support such a conjecture."

[77] It has been observed by K. Homann, *F.H. Jacobis Philosophie der Freiheit*. München 1973, pp. 51-54 and 265 that Jacobi's references to Spinoza are all taken from the *Tractatus theologico-politicus*. This seems to indicate that Jacobi's main interest is not metaphysical; rather the precise context for Jacobi's dealing with Spinoza must be seen in his preoccupation with the problem of freedom and despotism. Hence, because he is concerned first of all with political philosophy, he turns mainly to the *Tractatus*. In the ensuing debate on Spinozism, however, Jacobi also refers to the *Ethics*, etc. It is interesting to note that until then the neglect of *Ethics* had been typical of the 18th century's reception of Spinoza.

Morgenstunden, would present him as an advocate of Spinozism [echoes of such suppositions are found below pp. 108, 115-116, 140-142]. The roots of such misunderstandings might be sought in the curious fact that, when fighting against Spinozism, it is mainly against his own temptation that Jacobi is fighting.[78] His relationship to the kind of rational thinking exemplified by Spinoza is definitely a love-hate relationship. But Jacobi knew that, ultimately, rational thinking was taking him away from the personal God. That is why the commitment to rational thinking must end at one point, if one cares for truth and reality. "I extricate myself from the affair by a *salto mortale*."[88][79]

It might be surprising to hear Lessing say later in the conversation: "All in all, I find your *salto mortale* not bad.... Take me with you if that is possible." [96] But Lessing knows too well that he is not going to try the *salto mortale*. When invited by Jacobi to side with him and risk the leap he answers: "Even to do that [i.e., the very siding with Jacobi] would entail a leap I may no longer ask of my old legs and my muddled head." [96] Of these "last words" of Lessing Kierkegaard observes: "Here Lessing's irony beautifully reveals itself, since he is presumably aware that when one is to leap, one must be alone about it, and hence also alone about understanding its impossibility.... Although... the leap is itself the decision, Jacobi proposes to make something like a transition to it.... His [Lessing's] answer is therefore a jest. It is very far from being dogmatic; it is entirely correct dialectically, and it is personally evasive."[80]

The conversations of the Summer of 1780 had left a clear impression on Jacobi's mind. Three years later [July 21, 1783] he could write to Elise Reimarus the often quoted statement that "Lessing was in his final days a firm [entschiedener] Spinozist." [79] In November 1783, at the end of his report of the

---

[78] See Timm, *Gott und die Freiheit*, p. 146.

[79] Thus it is right to say with Timm, *Gott und die Freiheit*, p. 38: "Jacobi takes a constructive, but polemical interest in Lessing's Spinozism. It is expected to provide him with the springboard for his *salto mortale*."

[80] Kierkegaard, *Concluding*, pp. 93-94. Lessing and Kierkegaard represent two different perspectives on the "leap", though; for a highly sophisticated analysis of these differences see Michalson, *Lessing's "Ugly Ditch"*.

conversations, he qualified his statement somewhat: "... I knew beyond ~~a the~~ shadow of a doubt [entschieden] that 'Lessing does not believe in a cause of things which is distinct from the world'; or that 'Lessing is a Spinozist.'" [103] But in both cases the result was the same: because of what Jacobi understood by "Spinozist" his statement amounted to making Lessing into an atheist. The man from whom Jacobi had hoped to receive help against Spinoza had disqualified himself.

B/ Jacobi's eagerness to publish the content of his conversations with Lessing is first explained by him as a reaction to Mendelssohn's "premature" publication of his *Morgenstunden*. The relationship between Jacobi and Mendelssohn, for all its external civility, had become rather shifty in the fall of 1785. Their epistolary exchange is full of mis-understandings, even deceptions, intentional or not. Both seem to have practiced willful dissimulation and both ought to share equal guilt for the upcoming incidents. At the news of Mendelssohn's imminent publication, Jacobi understood that Mendelssohn had broken his promise not to publish anything about the content of their own correspondence without showing it to him first; he feared that Lessing and he would be misrepresented in their relation to Spinozism. In a strict sense Mendelssohn did not break his promise, but he did nothing to reassure Jacobi, who feared to be overtaken by Mendelssohn. And in a resolute manner Mendelssohn manoeuvered to get ahead of Jacobi: in his *Morgenstunden* he dealt with Lessing's Spinozism so as to neutralize in advance Jacobi's disclosure of Lessing's Spinozism and to forestall the impact of Jacobi's allegations. Therefore Jacobi was not totally wrong in his anticipations and he felt justified in publishing his "Spinoza letters." The outcome of this spectacle was that the *Morgenstunden* and *Über die Lehre des Spinoza* appeared practically at the same time.

If we look for less misty motives on Jacobi's part for going ahead with the publication of his book, we can say that he was eager to reveal the truth about Lessing and, politely, to denounce him as the unfortunate product of rationalism. In the last analysis he saw the publication of his report as part of a wider denunciation: that of rational theism and of German idealism, which both lead to atheism and from which the leap into faith can alone save. The publication of his book must therefore be seen in the larger context of Jacobi's lifelong concern: to oppose the inconsistent claims of those who think they can be both rationalists and theists, and attain a rational knowledge of the supranatural. "There can be no natural philosophy of the supranatural," [97] Jacobi counters.[81]

Mendelssohn spent the last weeks of his life preparing a massive rebuttal of Jacobi's book and in his *An die Freunde Lessings* threw indignant blame upon Jacobi. However, Jacobi's *Wider Mendelssohns Beschuldigungen* contained nothing like a withdrawal of his accusation. This book is the work of a besieged Jacobi and offers a sad mixture of arrogance, helpless pathos, and bad taste. When we reduce the book to its essential content, we hear Jacobi express his doubt as to whether Lessing's *Nathan*, his literary testament, can be viewed as a praise of providence [153] as Mendelssohn saw it. He would have us believe that Lessing had fallen into no small error [155] and questions that he was a real theist [152-153]: he rather used Christian theism as a cover for his esoteric pantheism. Wrongly, Jacobi claims to find in Th. Winzenmann a confirmation of his views.[82] He protests that he had not lied in his report. "I stand alone against a whole host...." [159][83] "Just let them go ahead and triumph over me! It is enough that they cannot triumph over my cause. It is enough that this very cause has taken a turn which could not be more instructive." [160] The abrupt, irritated tone is at the very least disturbing.[84] Occasionally Jacobi enlists Kant in his ranks [158][85] but this misuse prompted Kant to write a rectification,[86] on the one hand denouncing the risks of decrying

---

[81] See Bell, *Spinoza*, pp. 79-80.

[82] See Timm, *Gott und die Freiheit*, p. 264.

[83] Meaning especially Nicolai and his group, "la morgue berlinoise."

[84] Scholz, *Hauptschriften*, p. lxxcii remarks on "the lack of self-control and objectivity which makes Jacobi shrink back with touchiness in front of Mendelssohn at the very moment he sees further than Mendelssohn and is right against him. The consequence of that lack is an excessive cordiality on the one hand, and ungrounded touchiness on the other. Furthermore, a self-feeling appears that makes him totally incapable, in matters which are close to his heart and which he has taken into his head, to suffer other opinions even if they are well-founded. In fact he always speaks like a 'superintendent from heaven' [A. von Arnim] and has totally neglected Hegel's wisdom that a philosopher who wishes to make an impact must refrain from edifying."

[85] Quoting passages from the *Critique of Pure Reason* published in 1781.

[86] I. Kant, *What Does it Mean: To Orientate Oneself in Thinking?* 1786.

Schwärmerei

reason and the dangers of enthusiasm [Schwärmerei] released by Spinozism, and on the other, protesting his own innocence as regards the suspicion of Spinozism, which some might have found suggested by Jacobi.[87]

6. Mendelssohn and Lessing's Spinozism

We now turn to Mendelssohn who, in his *Morgenstunden*,[88] dealt with pantheism in three lectures, the last of which was devoted to the form of pantheism he claimed for Lessing: he called it "refined" [*geläuterter, verfeinerter*] pantheism. The concept of "refined pantheism" remains artificial throughout and betrays an intention of exculpating Lessing from the charge of atheism.[89] The concept would have received clearer contours had Mendelssohn been able to make it overlap with the less defensive concept of panentheism to express the immanence of the world in God. This he seemed unwilling to do. His "refined pantheism" amounted to a traditional theist position. To Spinozism he opposed his theism and seemingly rejected panentheism when he said: "We live, move, and are as effects of God, but not in him."[90] Whether Lessing's form of pantheism can be called panentheistic cannot be decided yet. My question here is rather about Mendelssohn's refined pantheism and it seems that it cannot be called panentheistic. At any rate Mendelssohn was convinced that one can espouse pantheism, or a refined form of it, without becoming married to Spinoza. He thought that refined pantheism "is totally compatible with the truths of religion and morality" [73]; that the difference which

---

[87] Before the alternative: faith or reason, Kant forges the hybrid concept of "Vernunftglaube" [rational faith] as a verbal compromise that this time, contrary to *Critique of Pure Reason* A 828f., indeed gives priority to reason; Jacobi will later call this hybrid concept a *contradictio in adjecto*.

[88] *Morgenstunden oder Vorlesungen über das Dasein Gottes*. Berlin 1785. In Scholz, *Hauptschriften*, pp. 1-44 [lectures xiii, xiv, xv].

[89] It is no surprise that Jacobi rejected the application to Lessing of the concept of "refined pantheism." "With the refined pantheism which he is to swallow for his healing, Lessing would only be a half head, according to my judgment. I am not going to let Mendelssohn educate him to that after his death." Jacobi's letter to E. Reimarus [November 7, 1785] in Scholz, *Hauptschriften*, p. xc.

[90] In Scholz, *Hauptschriften*, p. 5.

seems to set such pantheism apart from religion and morality "merely resides in an overly subtle speculation which [is] far from influencing human actions and happiness in the least."

Then in a *coup de théâtre* intended to demonstrate that, after all, Lessing had never shrunk from showing him his serious thoughts, Mendelssohn attempted to illustrate what he understood by "refined pantheism" with the help of Lessing's early fragment "The Christianity of Reason" [1751/53][91] [below 74-76, without nos. 6-12 which contain a speculative deduction of the Trinity]; Lessing had shown it to him at the time[92] and it had now been published by his brother [1784]. In it we find the following: God thinks himself in his perfection, and there we have the Son as image of God; God thinks his perfections individually, and there we have the world; the infinite series of created beings constitutes a harmony; their perfections are related to the perfections of God as parts to the whole. In other words, we find in the fragment the ideas of reduplication [better expressed in *The Education* § 73], of harmony, of immanence of things in God, of the "transcendental unity" of God with the world which Jacobi in his report correctly interpreted as the Spinozist *Hen kai Pan* or unity of *natura naturans* with *natura naturata* [101-102]. Mendelssohn's "objections" at the time Lessing had shown him the fragment might well have been directed at the panentheistic flavour of the essay and at the panentheistic interpretation Lessing was giving of the transcendental unity.[93] Now he finds the fragment to be an example of the "totally refined" twist Lessing was already giving to pantheism. This form of pantheism was called "refined" possibly because Mendelssohn thought it allowed for the objective existence of the manifold

---

[91] In *Werke* VII, pp. 278-281.

[92] Does it still represent the late Lessing's position? Altmann, *Mendelssohn*, p. 610 quotes a passage from Lessing's letter to Mendelssohn of May 1, 1774 [in Lachmann-Muncker 18, p. 110] in which he says: "My former fanciful ideas [Grillen] on this subject I still remember very well [= "The Christianity of Reason"], and I also remember the objections you raised against them, as a result of which I was at once dissuaded from taking them seriously myself henceforth." Altmann, however, comments that this is a typical statement of Lessing's and does not mean that he had abandoned those ideas completely.

[93] See Altmann, "Gespräch", p. 57 on Lessing's panentheistic interpretation of the transcendental unity as differing from Jacobi's.

outside God, posited by a free act of creation; or better, because the transcentendal unity constituted by God and the world does not exclude a kind of plurality, as Lessing explicitly said in *The Education* § 73.[94]

Mendelssohn knew more about Lessing's interest in Spinoza himself. In a letter of April 17, 1763[95] Lessing had expressed to him some of his ideas about Spinoza at a time when he was intensively reading the philosopher [Breslau 1760-1765]. This letter reproduces the fragment of the same year [without its first and last paragraphs] "From Spinoza Leibniz only came upon the Track of the Preestablished Harmony"[96] which contains Lessing's critical re-reading of Mendelssohn's *Philosophische Gespräche* of 1755. It is thought that Lessing had planned, in those years, to write a *Rettung* [rescue] of Spinoza[97] which would certainly not have failed to draw public attention, although it is hard to surmise that it would have produced the kind of scandal Jacobi's broadcast did. Mendelssohn answered the letter in May 1763[98] saying that Lessing's restrictions concerning the Spinoza-Leibniz filiation had not convinced him; he still believed that Spinoza, before Leibniz, had formulated the essential points of the preestablished harmony between mind and body, thought and extension, idea and things. There is no indication that Lessing changed his mind in the following years. Therefore it is surprising that Lessing said not a word when Jacobi asserted in July 1780: "Mendelssohn has clearly demonstrated that the *harmonia praestabilita* is to be found in Spinoza" [92]. At least we find no word that Jacobi thought advisable to report.

---

[94] E.A. Bergmann, *Hermaea. Studien zu G.E. Lessings theologischen und philosophischen Schriften*. Leipzig 1883, pp. 74-78 suggests that this vision of a unity that does not exclude a kind of plurality came to Lessing from Tertullian's reflections on God and the Trinity and on the relationship of God to the world. Thus, Bergmann submits, it is the thought-world of the Church Fathers which constitutes the sub-structure of the conversations with Jacobi [76] although the Fathers are nowhere mentioned by name.

[95] *Werke* VIII, pp. 719-720.

[96] *Werke* VIII, pp. 517-518, published only in 1795 by Lessing's brother along with "On the Reality of Things Outside God" under the general heading "Spinozisterei."

[97] H. Göbel in *Werke* VIII, pp. 718-719.

[98] *Werke* VIII, pp. 720-722.

Lessing's and Mendelssohn's letters of 1763 prompt two observations. First, Lessing had a precise knowledge of Spinoza, due especially to his readings in Breslau. Second, Mendelssohn knew of Lessing's interest in Spinoza, although he found it difficult to follow him. A further remark is made by Altmann and serves as a conclusion to his analysis of the documents just mentioned:[99] "In the philosophical debate with Mendelssohn... Lessing shows himself to be incomparatively more serious and thorough."

When Mendelssohn affirmed that Lessing was "on his way to link pantheistic concepts even with positive religion" [77], he could base his judgment on conversations, letters, and fragments similar to those mentioned up to now. He felt he knew enough of Lessing's pantheism to make such a statement with confidence. But had he taken into account another fragment of the same Breslau period, "On the Reality of Things Outside God"?[100] Yes, if we follow Altmann;[101] according to him the central question which the fragment discusses appears almost *verbatim* in the *Morgenstunden* where Mendelssohn has Lessing ask: "Must something be added to the thought of God if this thought is to become real outside God?"[102] Granting that Mendelssohn had seen the fragment, he had then been able to read in it such passages as: "I must confess that I can form no concept of the reality of things outside God.... If in the concept which God has of the reality of a thing everything is to be found that is found in its reality outside him, then both realities are one, and everything which is supposed to exist outside God exists in God." While it is not totally clear yet that here Lessing was linking "pantheistic concepts with positive religion," one thing is clear: to call this approach "refined pantheism" is a rather odd way of designating the panentheistic features of those speculative reflections.[103]

---

[99] Altmann, "Gespräch", pp. 50-53.

[100] *Werke* VIII, pp. 515-516, written in 1763.

[101] Altmann, "Gespräch", p. 55.

[102] In Scholz, *Hauptschriften*, p. 21.

[103] Altmann, "Gespräch", p. 55 emphasizes the panentheistic character of the present fragment and of the other writings we are presently reviewing. He also refers to a number of interpreters who have detected the same panentheistic element in Lessing's thought.

According to Bell, *Spinoza*, p. 32, before 1760 Lessing's writings show but thin

Finally, if one wants to consider all Spinoza-like statements that came to us from Lessing and were known to Mendelssohn, certain paragraphs in *The Education of the Human Race*[104] cannot be overlooked. The famous § 73 deserves special attention.[105] The speculative deduction of the trinitarian doctrine found there reemploys some ideas of "The Christianity of Reason" [ideas of immanence, reduplication, transcendental unity] as well as the image of the mirror already found at the end of "From Spinoza Leibniz only came upon the Track of the Preestablished Harmony."[106] Of

---

traces of Spinoza, traces that might be "the result of some contact with Spinoza's thought." However, he assumes on the next page that Lessing's "agreement with Spinoza on vital issues is proven." This is precisely what ought to be demonstrated. I find it difficult to see, in the documents reviewed above, apart from the idea of immanence, anything that is clearly suggestive of Spinoza. A relation to *Ethics* II, 10-12 and II, 45-49, postulated by A. Schilson, *Geschichte im Horizont der Vorsehung.* Mainz 1974, p. 216 can hardly be demonstrated, although I tend to agree with Schilson's general interpretation of Lessing's theism.

[104] In his *Morgenstunden* Mendelssohn refers to this "short piece of writing which [Lessing] published shortly before his death" [below p. 73].

[105] I know of no specific reference by Mendelssohn to § 73 of *The Education.* However, Mendelssohn's uneasiness with the general content of *The Education* is attested by his remarks in *Jerusalem oder über religiöse Macht und Judentum. Gesammelte Schriften.* Vol. 8, p. 162: he had no idea of an education of the human race in three stages of progressive revelation which, he says, "my late friend Lessing was led to imagine by I do not know which historian scholar of the human race." Mendelssohn must have repeatedly expressed this critical opinion to Lessing, which led Lessing to write in his last letter to Mendelssohn [December 19, 1780]: "I am not surprised that not everything I wrote recently has pleased you. Nothing at all was supposed to please you since nothing was written for you." In M. Mendelssohn, *Gesammelte Schriften.* Vol. 12.2: *Briefwechsel* II.2. 1976, p. 202 and in *LM* 18, p. 362.

[106] The parable of the mirror reads as follows [*Werke* VIII, p. 518]: "Would you allow me a parable? Two savages who for the first time see their image in a mirror. Once the amazement is passed, they begin to philosophize on this apparition. The image in the mirror, both say, makes precisely the same movements which a body makes, and it makes them in the same order. Consequently, conclude both, the sequence of movements of the image and the sequence of movements of the body must be explained by one and the same cause [Grund]." Lessing's text breaks here. Th.W. Danzel complemented the parable in the very plausible following manner [from Rilla, GW 10, pp. 368-369]: "The two savages will not agree on this one cause. The first one

this § 73 Jacobi said: "I would like to know how anyone can make sense of this passage without recourse to Spinozist ideas" [102].[107] Altogether, Jacobi was not in a position to consider that the exaggerated insistence on the extra-mundane existence of God, taken to its limit, runs the risk of positing the world outside God; he could not see that the denial of the extra-mundane God became far less problematic when it was affirmed, in the same breath, that the world exists in God and not outside God. But for Lessing, the assumption that things exist *also* outside God is "an unnecessary, as well as extravagant reduplication of the primeval image [Urbild]."[108]

It is probable that Mendelssohn knew all those ideas of Lessing's[109] when he began writing his *Morgenstunden*. He wished to make clear to all, against Jacobi's innuendos, that he had "pursued philosophical discourse with Lessing for quite some time; for years we exchanged views on such topics, with an ingenuous love of truth, which precluded dogmatism as well as false

---

will say: My body and the image in the mirror, these are two autonomous movements, which a hidden power has arranged in such a way, though, that they have to agree. This would be Leibniz' view. The second one will say: There is just one movement, nevertheless in two kinds of manifestation. That would be Spinoza's view."

[107] Curiously, Jacobi has not tried to understand § 73 in the framework of a philosophical interpretation of the trinitarian doctrine as found in the Nicene Creed, although the latter seems to be Lessing's point of departure. Timm, *Gott und die Freiheit*, p. 122 is right in recalling that evidence. "Due to the Jacobi-Mendelssohn controversy, scholarship fell into the wrong track as though the point would be to trace the theorem back to Spinoza or Leibniz" instead of tracing it back to its Christian source.

[108] *Werke* VIII, p. 516.

[109] He might even have felt some implicit pointer to Spinoza's doctrine and person in the main character of Lessing's *Nathan*. K.S. Guthke suggests such a connection in his "Lessing und das Judentum", *WSA* IV [1977] 229-271, esp. 250-256. The independence of ethical praxis from positive religion is common to both characters. Both serve an ethical ideal which does not need to be coupled with an eudemonist reference to transcendence.

One can still prefer to see Mendelssohn behind the figure of Nathan; then it can be recalled that Lessing saw Mendelssohn himself as "a second Spinoza" [letter to Michaelis, October 16, 1754 in *Werke* II, pp. 646-647]. For its part, Guthke's suggestion goes as far as to perceive behind the hero of Lessing's early play *Die Juden* [1749] the figure of the selfsame Spinoza.

deference." [66] On the basis of that prolonged community of thought he believed he could claim for Lessing the position he called "refined pantheism."

Mendelssohn reiterated his views on Lessing's thought in his *An die Freunde Lessings*.[110] By then the polemic with Jacobi had become extremely bitter. Mendelssohn "presented himself and Judaism as being in complete accord with the Enlightenment, and Jacobi and Christianity as submitting to a *sacrificium intellectus*.... He saw in Jacobi another Lavater in disguise."[111] Unfortunate undertones appear, for instance, when Mendelssohn declares that he could not have been expected to withdraw his friendship from Lessing when he "saw in him an adherent of the Jew, Baruch Spinoza. The label of Jew and Spinozist could be for me in no way so startling or so grating as it would seem to be for Herr Jacobi." [130]

I have already quoted at length from *An die Freunde Lessings*. It will suffice here to formulate what its specific emphasis seems to have been. Whereas the *Morgenstunden* defended Lessing against the accusation of being an atheist and constituted a "first rescue" of Lessing as refined pantheist, we find in *An die Freunde Lessings* an effort to present Lessing as a defender of theism against the insinuation that he had been a blasphemer and a hypocrite. Mendelssohn's second work has adequately been called a "second rescue" of Lessing.[112]

I am willing to agree with Scholz[113] in considering Mendelssohn, compared with Jacobi, as "the more skilled interpreter" of *Lessing*.

---

[110] M. Mendelssohn, *An die Freunde Lessings*. Berlin 1786. In Scholz, *Hauptschriften*, pp. 283-325.

[111] Altmann, *Mendelssohn*, p. 635. Lavater, then a "deacon" [i.e., second preacher] in Zürich, was the one who had challenged Mendelssohn in 1769 either to refute C. Bonnet's demonstration of the truth of Christianity or to convert! See *Werke*, VII, pp. 713 and 976-977. - However, I am not totally convinced by Altmann's assertion that Jacobi tried to convert Mendelssohn to Christianity. As Bell, *Spinoza*, p. 85 argues, he was no more seeking to convert Mendelssohn than he was to libel Lessing; rather, "he was endeavouring to discredit rationalism and the Enlightenment."

[112] H. Göbel in *Werke* VIII, pp. 748-749.

[113] Scholz, *Hauptschriften*, p. lxvii; see also pp. xiii and xc.

His familiarity with Lessing made Jacobi's insinuation as to Lessing's secret atheism, and "shallow-minded" atheism at that [132], simply intolerable to him. Therein Mendelssohn showed a better understanding of Lessing's puzzling tactic of advocating certain positions for the sake of exercise and in order to have the issues debated. However, it seems to me that Jacobi had the deeper understanding of *Spinozism*, not Mendelssohn. Furthermore, we must recognize that, in the long run, Jacobi saw better the threat hanging over the Enlightenment and the nascent German idealism, and the ultimate dangers of rationalism. In that light Mendelssohn's last writings mark "the end of religious Enlightenment" [114] whereas Jacobi's critique earned him a prophetic place in the history of modern philosophy.

Now, was *Lessing's Spinozism* better understood by Mendelssohn or by Jacobi? To define the real "spirit of Spinoza" has often been a vexed question and this is not the place to decide on the correctness of any Spinoza interpretation. What Spinoza thought is not under discussion here; rather what Jacobi and Mendelssohn made of him. What they made of him resulted in two distinct concepts of Spinozism, each of which being forced upon Lessing's work with less and less regard for what Lessing had really thought.

It must be emphasized again that Jacobi's conception of Spinoza did not overlap with Lessing's. Jacobi's report of his conversations with Lessing frankly witnesses to major discrepancies. In contrast with Jacobi's Spinoza "Lessing refuses neither reality nor thinking to the *natura naturans*.... God and world according to Lessing are two aspects of the same reality... but God's transcendental unity suppresses neither his reality not his thought," says Altmann.[115] Nevertheless, I would like to see such a statement demonstrated in detail. Jacobi had done his best to instruct Lessing in his own interpretation of Spinoza, without winning his approval. In return, Jacobi began to force upon the late Lessing his radical view of Spinozism, as became clear in the controversy with Mendelssohn. In his correspondence with Mendelssohn he returned to the task and produced a number of dissertations on Spinozism that left Mendelssohn perplexed; the more he listened to Jacobi, the more

---

[114] Timm, *Gott und die Freiheit*, p. 362.
[115] Altmann, "Gespräch", pp. 57-58.

confused he became [125, 142, 146].[116] Mendelssohn often referred
to his inability to enter into thought forms that would deviate from
the Leibniz-Wolffian tradition which provided him with the
categories for reading Spinoza. The reading of Jacobi's account of
his conversations with Lessing had already left him bewildered; as
Jacobi reported it, Mendelssohn could not follow Lessing's
argumentation too well. He had his difficulties with Spinozism
which he considered too subtle an expression of pantheism while
Jacobi found pantheism best expressed in Spinoza. This is not to
say that Mendelssohn misunderstood Lessing, however; only that he
did not share his opinion and wished to keep him away from a
gross form of pantheism. Throughout this curious *pas de deux* one
cannot help thinking that Jacobi's concept of Spinozism, right or
wrong, is more coherent than both Mendelssohn's and Lessing's,
while for the three of them clarity seems to be a rare commodity.

X   The situation could be assessed as follows: Jacobi maximized
Lessing's Spinozism while Mendelssohn minimized it. Total light is
still missing, though, and we find ourselves thrown back into a
labyrinth. One way out of it is suggested by Altmann's study of
these complex issues and helps explain Mendelssohn's perplexity
[and ours as well]. Altmann concludes his solid analysis of the
questions concerning Lessing's Spinozism[117] by stating, in
agreement with a good number of interpreters, that Lessing was
pondering a panentheistic interpretation of Spinoza's system. Why
does this help us understand Mendelssohn's feeling of confusion?
First, panentheism as a philosophical position does not seem to
have attracted his favour; but it is the position he would like to
claim for his friend Lessing although he finds Lessing's
argumentation as reported by Jacobi, over and above Lessing's
exposés to him, unconvincing. Second, Mendelssohn is not directly
interested in Spinozism for lack of connaturality with the system;
personally, he is above all interested in the issues of pantheism.
Only rarely does he apply the expression "refined Spinozism" to the
thought of Lessing: he prefers the expression "refined pantheism".
Being ill at ease with both Spinozism and panentheism, he stuck to
the expression "refined pantheism" to describe Lessing's deepest
tendency. On the basis of Lessing's fragments and correspondence

---

[116] See Altmann, "Gespräch", p. 28.

[117] Altmann, "Gespräch", pp. 40-58.

which we reviewed earlier, it appears that "panentheism" would have been more accurate. If we accept this label for Lessing's searching speculations, then Jacobi and Mendelssohn can quietly be left turning Lessing's pantheism round to suit their own views,[118] and we can proceed to a direct consideration of Lessing's panentheism.

---

[118] Who has understood whom? Did Jacobi or Lessing better understand Spinoza? did Mendelssohn or Jacobi better understand Lessing? Although my study suggests a certain answer to these vexed questions, it is tempting to extend to Mendelssohn what Kierkegaard applies to Jacobi and to say of both in regard to Lessing what Kierkegaard reports of Hegel's friend: "Hegel is also supposed to have died with the words upon his lips, that there was only one man who had understood him, and he has misunderstood him...." *Concluding*, p. 65 note.

In his analysis of the Spinoza controversy D. Bell, *Spinoza in Germany*, pp. 71-96 is not quite willing to acknowledge Jacobi's contribution toward the Spinoza renaissance of the 1780s. I find this reluctance unfortunate. Doubtless more to the point, Bell believes that both Mendelssohn and Jacobi seriously misunderstood Spinoza: the former by neglecting Spinoza's ethics, the latter by reducing Spinoza to Leibniz and Wolff. Lessing, Herder, and Goethe would have understood him better although none of them saw himself as an interpreter of Spinoza; they rather assimilated creatively some of Spinoza's ideas [p. 148] and were primarily investing their energies in sketching their own answers to their own questions.

In his still very readable work, *Lessing als Theologe*. Halle 1854, C. Schwarz tended to play down Lessing's debt to Spinoza. He concluded his section on Lessing's Spinozism with the spirited lines [p. 97]: "Lessing did not teach refined Spinozism, as his too weak defender Mendelssohn conceded, any more than he adhered to a quite ordinary one, as Jacobi claimed. He took the defence of Spinoza only because the latter was attacked; with skepticism he opposed the tempestuous Jacobi who was knocking down everything with his newly discovered faith-instance! All in all, in doing so, Lessing was merely standing for the cause of thinking as such and of its unrestricted right! In fact his concepts of God and the world were totally different from Spinoza's; it is only in opposition to the orthodox representation of the divinity, which he found entirely insipid, that Lessing sided for a moment with the much decried philosopher."

7. Lessing's Panentheism[119]

Is it correct to say that Lessing propounded a panentheistic view? Is Lessing's "refined pantheism" better called panentheism?[120] Has Lessing only held an immanence of things in God, as Mendelssohn would have claimed for him,[121] or did he also believe in a "secret immanence of God's spirit in man's spirit," as Scholz seems to think?[122] That Lessing "surely stood closer to Spinoza than Mendelssohn assumed"[123] can be granted. Yet is the statement warranted that "a divinity active through the order of the world, as stood before Lessing's eyes [especially in *The Education*], is indeed certainly divinity enough to be able to count as a 'cause of things distinct from the world'"?[124] Could Lessing's longed-for alternative to "orthodox concepts" of the divinity be satisfied with a mere verbal solution, aimed at overcoming of the supranaturalist representation of a God "flying over" the order of the world? Did it not also require a total dissolution of God into the world in the sense of *deus sive natura* according to which "God" is only another name for "world"?

There seems to be no question that Lessing believed in a divinity active throughout the order of the world. But this belief as

---

[119] W. Dilthey, *Das Erlebnis*, pp. 164-165 and 172 already spoke in 1867 of "Lessing's panentheism" in his effort to rescue him from the rationalist tendencies of the *Aufklärung* and to bring him into proximity with Leibniz. See also M. Haug, *Entwicklung und Offenbarung bei Lessing*. Gütersloh 1928, p. 98.

[120] W. Gericke, *Sechs theologische Schriften G.E. Lessings*. Berlin 1985 [following the suggestion of H. Schultze, *Lessings Toleranzbegriff*. Göttingen 1969, p. 110 ff.] takes up the thesis that Lessing stood in the so-called spiritualist tradition of thinkers such as S. Frank, Paracelsus, V. Weigel, J. Böhme, J.K. Dippel and J.C. Edelmann. The spiritualist tradition would be characterized by a concept of faith that downplays a connection with the church and by the proximity to God of a human subject not in need of a mediator in order to be born again and saved. Gericke's study, whatever we think of its demonstrative value and of the merit of chasing one's forefathers and precursors in the family tree of intellectual history, clearly indicates that Lessing's *Hen kai Pan* does not immediately and exclusively call for a Spinozist interpretation.

[121] See Scholz, *Hauptschriften*, p. xiii.

[122] Scholz, *Hauptschriften*, pp. lxix-lxx.

[123] Scholz, *Hauptschriften*, p. lxix; see p. xiii.

[124] Scholz, *Hauptschriften*, p. lxxii.

such cannot be called panentheistic: it is part and parcel of every theism. Panentheism denotes immanence of things in God. This view did not appeal to Mendelssohn personally but he seems to have claimed it for his friend Lessing under a different name. How is this to be understood?

We must here consider what is currently called panentheism and gauge the extent to which it can be found in Lessing's thought. Panentheism as a way of thinking of God steers a course between theism and pantheism. On this count already it provides an alternative to both supranaturalist theism and Spinozist pantheism, which might have been the object of Lessing's searching reflections. In order to avoid the pitfalls of both theism and pantheism, panentheism postulates a dipolar nature of the divinity according to which God, through his relative aspect, includes the world and, through his absolute aspect, is distinct from the world.[125] In its perfect form it consists of five factors found simultaneously: God is eternal, he is capable of change, he is self-aware, he knows the world, he includes the world [not in his essence but in his actuality]. In other words, the Supreme Being is seen as eternal-temporal consciousness, knowing and including the world. Obviously, accounting for the simultaneous presence of the noted five factors in God is not without its conceptual difficulties. Does panentheism represent more than a verbal solution to the lasting antinomies that plague our thinking of God?

Exponents of panentheism are well aware of such difficulties; but these are unavoidable in dealing with a supremely complex problem. - Who are these exponents? Among the most significant representatives of panentheism in various traditions we can name: Schelling, Berdyaev, Whitehead, Iqbal, and Radhakrishnan. The main concern of these thinkers, and the concern of process philosophers and theologians in general, is to think of God in a way that does not reduce what happens in the contingent world to a matter of indifference to God, and that expresses the central insights of religious consciousness. In the Christian tradition, for example, the central themes of the "suffering God" and of "*deus est caritas*" clearly indicate that God is not taken to be indifferent to the world, while his including the world is implied by Paul's words that

---

[125] See C. Hartshorne and W.L. Reese, *Philosophers Speak of God*. Chicago 1953, p. 15.

"in him we live, move, and are" [*Acts* 17:28][126] and by his insistent statement that we live "in Christo." Does not the formula, "The world in God" merely state the other side of the belief in "God in the world" [Incarnation]?

I wish to submit that, in his dealing with the problem of the God-world relationship and with Spinoza, Lessing did not specifically envisage a panentheistic solution. But he did tend toward it. Two observations seem to justify this statement. First, Lessing registers a disagreement with Spinoza on the crucial point that distinguishes pantheism from panentheism: whereas Spinoza had given up the idea of the contingency of the world[127] and posited the world as a necessary modification of the Substance, Lessing felt pressed to talk of "contingencies" in the being of God [as witnessed by his fragment, "On the Reality of Things Outside God"], thus challenging both Spinoza and an essential tenet of supranaturalist theism. In the same fragment he argued for God's reality, his thinking, and his including the world. We recall further that *The Education* § 73 adds a radical correction to Spinoza's central concept and says that God's "transcendental unity" "includes a kind of plurality." All this indicates that Lessing was drawing near to a panentheistic position.

Second, to a large extent Lessing's difficulties with the "orthodox concepts of the divinity" speak of his concern to think of God as more involved in the affairs of the world than the traditional concepts of theism would have it. Lessing detects a more adequate view in classical Antiquity. The human face of God strongly shines through the "authentic spirit of Antiquity"; in it God does not have the static and impassive features of an Assyrian satrap but has real passions; and he is a participant in the universe. The Prometheus poem had something of such a divine-human shimmer. Lessing "found it good." Again here *The Education* seems to depart from the idea of a God inaccessible to the influence of the world. He goes so far as to transfer into God himself the vision of the plurality of conflicting religious claims and of too imperfect a world; for, according to the idea of

---

[126] "The basic formula for the dynamic theology of identity of the time of Goethe" and "... for Christian Spinozism." Timm, *Gott und die Freiheit*, pp. 171 and 193.

[127] See Hartshorne-Reese, *Philosophers*, pp. 189-194.

"education", God's revelation itself submits to a progressive series of steps.[128]

In his tendency toward a panentheistic position Lessing is clear-headed enough to stay away from rhapsodic or enthusiastic effusions which, ultimately, would level the blatant differences between theism and Spinozist pantheism. He has as little intention of throwing overboard theism *per se*, as he has of blindly embracing pantheism in its Spinozist form. He treads a fine line between rejection and reception. His sympathy for Spinoza falls short of swallowing the hard pill which Spinoza prescribes for the belief in a personal God. His opposition to both orthodoxy and neology is ruthless as regards the latter, but differentiated as regards the former; he knows that he has to recover a number of orthodox elements he too quickly rejected.[129] Lessing is not the man to cast out definitely, without examination, nor to trivialize serious differences in the way we occasionally find represented in Mendelssohn and Goethe. Mendelssohn's poignant but not totally convincing lyricism in a passage of the *Morgenstunden* [65] might have provoked a certain embarrassment on the part of Lessing. It reads: "... Due to a misinterpretation of one and the same metaphor [= of the source and the river] at times God is placed too figuratively in the world, at times the world is placed too figuratively in God.... Do without words, friend of wisdom," Mendelssohn addresses the reader familiar with Leibniz and Wolff, "and embrace thy brother"; here Spinoza is undialectically interpreted as a brother-friend of the Leibniz-Wolffian doctrine which Mendelssohn still considered to owe a fundamental debt to Spinoza. We find an equally inadequate way of levelling differences in Goethe. Lessing might have been ready to accept Goethe's aphorism that "as poet and artist I am a polytheist, but as natural

---

[128] See Timm, *Gott und die Freiheit*, p. 78.

[129] See his letter to Mendelssohn, January 9, 1771 in *Werke* VII, pp. 879-881: "... [From a distance I see] certain truths that for a long time I had no longer considered such. Indeed my concern, more than one day old, is that, while I was throwing away certain prejudices, I threw away along with them a little too much, which I will have to recover. If I have not already started to do so, it is because I was hindered by the fear of dragging back all the garbage step by step into the house. It is infinitely difficult to know when and where to stop, and for more than one, reflection ends when they get tired of reflection."

scientist I am a pantheist, and the one as decidedly as the other. If I need a God for my personality as moral being, this is also taken care of [= I am a theist]."[130] But I doubt that he would have been able to subscribe to Goethe's enthusiastic statement concerning Spinozism: "It does not prove the existence [Dasein] of God, existence is God. And if others rebuke it on this ground for being atheistic [*atheum*], I would like to call and praise it as very theistic [*theissimum*] and very Christian [*christianis-simum*]."[131] Lessing is never seen glossing over difficulties or differences in so benign a manner.

I am more inclined to follow Mendelssohn when he declares that Lessing "was on his way to link pantheistic concepts even with positive religion." [77] The formulation is vague. But it says enough to indicate that Lessing was heading toward panentheism. That panentheism tends to unite pantheist elements with concepts received from positive religion should not be questioned if one keeps in mind that it lies somewhere between pantheism and theism. The link-up is possible provided we are not confronted with extreme forms of pantheism and theism. One cannot see how panentheism would be unacceptable to positive religion, since it seems to cohere with religious feelings and to be well anchored in normative scriptures. Therefore I accept Mendelssohn's statement concerning Lessing's "refined pantheism," which I would like to say of Lessing's panentheism: "This linking [of positive religion] is in fact as possible with pantheism as with the Ancients' system of emanation which, throughout the centuries, was accepted by religion and held to be the only orthodox doctrine." [77] The analogy with the emanationist doctrine is very much to the point since its roots are found in proximity to all forms of pantheism. The idea of emanation was certainly not easier to integrate with the tenets of positive religion than a theology which gives its preference to immanence.

---

[130] *Goethes Werke*. Sect. IV, Vol. 23. Weimar 1900, p. 226 [letter of January 6, 1813 to Jacobi].

[131] In Scholz, *Hauptschriften*, p. cviii. For the origin of such an exalted view of Spinoza in L. Schmidt and J. Jelles, see Timm, *Gott und die Freiheit*, pp. 162-163.

8. The Lasting Ambivalence of Lessing's Thought

The publication, in 1785, of Jacobi's account of his conversations with Lessing issued in the pantheism debate that gave its stamp to the philosophy of religion of the time of Goethe,[132] and showed the measure of the impact of Lessing's philosophical and theological legacy. The very ambivalence of Lessing's statements fed the debate then and continues to challenge the skills of interpreters. The history of interpretation shows that Jacobi has not been alone in reading Lessing as a Spinozist. Christian theology has generally been cool about a close association with Lessing, partly because of the Spinozist leanings which some of his utterances betray. As mentioned earlier, Spinozism has indeed been the Trojan horse introduced into the citadel of Lessing's literary production to discredit it and make it inadmissible to traditional religious thought. Only with reluctance were some professional theologians ready to pay serious attention to Lessing's religious thought as a whole and to its original contribution.

Such reluctance was only reinforced by the quite uninhibited manner in which atheist circles appropriated Lessing. Dialectical materialism, the self-appointed heir and "perfecter" of Spinoza not only tended to overlook the ambivalence of Spinoza himself; it also took Lessing's relation to Spinoza to be quite undialectical. Such appropriation is exemplified by the work of P. Rilla[133] who, taking issue with "bourgeois" Lessing scholarship, subscribes to Schopenhauer's view of pantheism as being "courtly [höflich] atheism."[134] Rilla cannot help wondering at "how close to the

---

[132] I am referring here to the title of H. Timm's work, *Gott und die Freiheit. Studien zur Religionsphilosophie der Goethezeit.* 1974.

    The lasting significance of Spinoza and of the late 18th century Spinoza renaissance has been pointedly formulated by Hegel: "When one enters the field of philosophy, one must first be Spinozist. The soul must take a bath in that ether of the one Substance in which everything that one has held for true is absorbed." *Sämtliche Werke.* Vol. 19. Stuttgart 1959, p. 376.

[133] P. Rilla was the East German editor of Lessing's *Gesammelte Werke.* Berlin 1954-1958, and the author of a biography of Lessing which he left unfinished at his death in 1954; it was published in 1958 and included as volume 10 of the *Gesammelte Werke* [hereafter *GW* 10].

[134] Rilla, *GW* 10, p. 367.

purely materialistic, purely atheistic conception"[135] Spinoza's pantheism stands, and celebrates Lessing as one who had the talent to approximate "a materialistic conception of the world to the extent it was at all possible on the basis of an idealistic philosophy."[136] Lessing recognized himself in the philosophy of Spinoza [137] and he is said to have shared with him, among other things, the view of the unity of spirit and matter.[138] Lessing's exoteric writings [that is, for Rilla, his theological essays] should not lead us astray here: their esoteric/philosophical content amounts to a philosophical destruction, a dumping over of all theological conceptions, Christian and biblical alike.[139]

In order for the Marxist conquest of Lessing's terrain to be complete, clarity had to be assumed where there is none or where there is only penumbra. As a first step, Spinoza was to be brought to heel; as a second, Lessing's distance to Spinoza had to be denied and his tendency toward panentheism ignored. Sporadic statements by Lessing were to be hypostatized and taken to warrant a confident affirmation of his Spinozist world-view.

It cannot be denied that many of Lessing's views present similarities with Spinozist conceptions, and his concept of God must be included among those views: Lessing might have developed it while reading Spinoza. A certain congeniality seems to exist between Lessing and Spinoza; besides their common anti-anthropomorphism in thinking of God, they share the same predilection for looking at the Bible in terms of eternal verities; they attach the same importance to praxis and to right behaviour as opposed to right belief; their efforts in the realm of rational ethic overlap considerably; they extol John's gospel and letters. Their ways of thinking converge on important points and perhaps it is by Lessing that Spinoza was least misunderstood during the late 18th century Spinoza craze. Clearly, they have much in common. But they are not identical. The central debate on whether Lessing

---

[135] Rilla, *GW* 10, p. 366.

[136] Rilla, *GW* 10, p. 371.

[137] Rilla, *GW* 10, p. 388.

[138] Rilla, *GW* 10, p. 370.

[139] Rilla, *GW* 19, pp. 372-375. See also Rilla's "Vorbemerkungen des Herausgebers", *Gesammelte Werke*, Vol. 1, p. 31.

conceived of God as transcendent or totally immanent continues. In that debate more and more attention is given to the entire work of Lessing in the firm conviction that there is no reason to over-emphasize sporadic Spinoza-like statements encountered here and there.

Indeed, Lessing's Spinoza-like statements do not give us a coherent picture of Spinoza. Should H. Regner win over our final assent when he studies all references, explicit and implicit, to Spinoza in Lessing's work and concludes with a Spinozist Lessing? What then? One could also reduce Lessing to Leibniz with equal "success".[140] And quite strikingly, a kind of "elective affinity" [Wahlverwandtschaft] between Lessing and Tertullian was discovered and demonstrated by E.A. Bergmann.[141] For his part, resting his analysis on a study of Lessing's entire life-work, A. Schilson[142] could demonstrate Lessing's belief in providence; it could well be argued that this belief must be upheld against Lessing's casual and late Spinozist utterances.

Be that as it may, because of the great versatility of his intelligence and the many-sidedness of his discourse, all attempts at identifying Lessing with a great predecessor [be it Spinoza, Leibniz, or Tertullian] are doomed to failure. As Bell says,[143] "the underlying character of his thought makes it impossible to tie him to one system. His philosophy was never fixed, but a restless movement in constant search of truth, a quest in which, we are told in *Eine Duplik* [Rejoinder], lies man's true worth."

Lessing was a reader of Spinoza, of course, as he was a reader of many other authors. We are to expect that fruits of his readings will appear here and there in his writings. Thus elements of Spinoza, Leibniz, and Tertullian can be identified in various places of Lessing's work. But to look for [and find!] a full-fledged alien system embedded in the very fabric of Lessing's work, would betray

---

[140] See, among others, H.E. Allison, *Lessing and the Enlightenment*. Ann Arbor 1966, pp. 66-79.

[141] E.A. Bergmann, *Hermaea. Studien zu G.E. Lessings theologischen und philosophischen Schriften*. Leipzig 1883, pp. 58-136, here p. 124.

[142] A. Schilson, *Geschichte im Horizont der Vorsehung*. Tübingen 1974.

[143] Bell, *Spinoza*, p. 86.

a serious misunderstanding of his personality. Rather, we may expect to find elements received from outside, transferred into the flow of his active search and thereby recast. Thus "Spinoza's insights were absorbed to re-emerge in a form characteristic of Lessing's genius."[144]

In the enterprise of interpreting Lessing's entire work the hunt for his predecessors has but a limited value. Granted, it is of some import to be able to assert that Lessing was closer to Spinoza than to Leibniz.[145] But why not one day study Lessing on his own terms? and why not, in such a study, look at Lessing's entire corpus and not only at his most baffling essays and fragments?

Much painstaking work is entailed in the requirement that Lessing's entire corpus be taken into consideration in order to arrive at a valid statement of his theological position. The very structure of his thought has to be brought out, within which, among other things, the incidental or unspecific references to Spinoza can be interpreted. Such a structure manifests itself not only in Lessing's more philosophical writings; it is at work as well in his entire artistic production. At this point it will suffice to indicate that the structure of Lessing's thought and work is such that in it the theatrical element plays a determining role. We shall return to this decisive element.

General conclusions on Lessing's "real" position are risky and should be avoided. This applies eminently to Lessing's conversations with Jacobi. Even Scholz' statement in favour of Lessing's theism, for all its competence and sophistication, is quite debatable. He can well write:

> Whoever, with Jacobi, makes this untiring God-seeker [Lessing] into an atheist because he meets with Spinoza in certain respects, has understood neither Spinoza, nor Lessing, but has in fact only demonstrated that he confuses the recognition of the highest Being with the reception of certain representations of the Highest Being which have been

---

144 Bell, *Spinoza*, p. 93.
145 Bell, *Spinoza*, p. 93.

developed in a certain cultural circle under the influence of a certain conception of life.[146]

But one remains divided between the fine discernment of the second part of the statement and the all-too-decisive character of its first part. One also keeps wondering whether too much or too little conclusiveness is attributed to Jacobi's account of Lessing's position. H. Göbel's statement is helpful here in that it affords the necessary hermeneutical caution:

> In no way would it be acceptable to consider such a conversation, composed [aufgezeichnetes] by somebody else and in addition held on their first encounter, to be, as it were, Lessing's last word on this topic, and still less so since similar statements are found neither in his printed writings, nor in his posthumous ones, nor even in letters or other transmitted conversations.[147]

Once all this has been said, it should be clear, though, that Jacobi has rendered a great service to intellectual history in making public the content of his conversations with Lessing and in expressing his misgivings as to the evolution of German philosophy. The events around Wolfenbüttel 1780 were most instructive; they would have remained unknown, had Jacobi kept silent. Their publication kindled the pantheism debate whose issues are of universal interest and are still with us. In the course of the debate German Enlightenment became aware of its endangered situation[148] and saw the peril of its being engulfed in dehumanizing rationalism. Lessing's friends did their best to rescue him from the debâcle. We can debate whether they succeeded. Nevertheless Jacobi had sounded the alarm. To quote the words of Dilthey,[149] Jacobi saw as a threat the fact that "on the clear day of critical rationalism the shadow of Spinoza, the great pantheist, began to lurk"; he shouted his concern about the return of the spectre. He might have overstated the case in denouncing Lessing as a victim of excessive

---

[146] Scholz, *Hauptschriften*, p. lxxiv.

[147] In *Werke* VIII, p. 749.

[148] See Blumenberg, *Arbeit*, p. 463.

[149] W. Dilthey, *Gesammelte Schriften*. Vol. XV. Göttingen 1970, p. 22.

rationalism, but the cry of alarm should have been taken seriously. Events since then have shown that Jacobi's critique had something prophetic about it and that "reason in its execution runs into an absolutism of identity which makes all other absolutisms undistinguishable."[150] The question remains whether the kind of rationalism denounced by Jacobi can be attributed to Lessing or whether Lessing himself can be said to have afforded a corrective to the consequent rationalism Jacobi saw in Spinozism.[151]

9. A Key-Text?

Finally, I wish to discuss briefly the question whether the Spinoza conversations, as reported by Jacobi, can be considered to be a key-text for the interpretation of Lessing. I think they cannot. Lessing's utterances in the course of those conversations, even if they are supplemented by his other sporadic statements in regard to Spinoza, do not amount to a coherent picture of a philosophical position that could be called Spinozist; still less do they amount to a clear representation of the fundamental thrust of Lessing's thought. I do not believe that they offer a sufficient basis for a decisive statement of what his search was about. The Spinoza conversations are certainly useful for understanding the first crisis of the German Enlightenment. In a general interpretation of Lessing himself they are not usable.[152]

---

[150] Blumenberg, *Arbeit*, p. 450.

[151] Could we not find the secret of Lessing's friendship toward Jacobi in the sympathy he felt for the dethronement of reason aimed at by Jacobi in favour of feeling and experience? This would mean that Lessing, as it were, had already abandoned the stance of the Enlightenment.

[152] For a similar view see H. Schultze in *Lessing und Spinoza*. Ed. by Th. Höhle. Halle 1982, p. 110. See also Dilthey, *Das Erlebnis*, p. 114.

  What J. Schneider, *Lessing's Stellung zur Theologie vor der Herausgabe der Wolfenbütteler Fragmente*. 's-Gravenhage 1953 [as found in G. and S. Baur, eds., *G.E. Lessing*. Darmstadt 1968, pp. 287-301] said concerning the use of Lessing's fragments should also be extended to the "fragment" left by Jacobi: "It sometimes appears as though 19th and 20th century scholars wanted to understand Lessing better than he understood himself. Lessing's many unfinished attempts at solving a problem that concerned him are being complemented 'in the spirit of Lessing.' Many Lessing scholars cannot resist the temptation of weighing the fragmentary writings of Lessing

Can we think of another writing that would function as a key-text? *The Education of the Human Race* comes immediately to mind and it is certain that it represents a careful statement of Lessing's views held through a long period of his maturity. But was it his final statement? Although his admirers were inclined to look at this writing as the spiritual testament of Lessing,[153] Lessing himself seems to have been reluctant to attach such importance to *The Education*. This impression would be partially confirmed by an "anecdote" which is reported by K.A. Böttinger[154] in 1838 and goes back to 1795, the date of his conversations with Elise Reimarus. The latter is said to have declared that "Lessing himself at the time when he published his *Education of the Human Race* did not believe any more in that dream earlier dreamt [= the dream of a progress toward higher humanity to be achieved through the advent of the age of the Spirit], but that he had published it then merely to make a diversion to the theological controversies." This anecdote might say more about Elise Reimarus' own disillusionment than about Lessing's; her role in the exchange between Jacobi and Mendelssohn had been less than successful and the knightly contest she was hoping to trigger between her two friends had turned into the most bitter clash. At any rate it invites caution and makes it difficult to consider *The Education* as Lessing's final word without further ado.

Lessing seems to have been the first one to relativize the import of *The Education* when he wrote:[155]

---

as though he had thought and written them in their complete form. Thus there is no end to guessing and fancying. However, it is more natural to assume that Lessing, while writing down his thoughts, saw the road blocked that could have provided him with a satisfactory solution and, not by accident, let the essays remain fragments." [p. 293] Fragments are fragments, and the way they were made known to us adds still more to their fragile reliability: Karl Lessing who preferred to see in his brother a rationalist, quite arbitrarily selected, among the papers left over, those that fitted his view of his brother's 'mode of thinking' [see p. 301, addition of 1967].

[153] See *Werke* VIII, p. 709.

[154] In Daunicht, *Lessing*, p. 465.

[155] Letter of April 6, 1778 to J.A.H. Reimarus, *Werke* VIII, p. 608.

>The Education of the Human Race is written by a
>good friend who likes to put forward all kinds of
>hypotheses and systems just for the pleasure of
>tearing them up again. The present hypothesis would
>indeed considerably shift the goal my Unknown
>envisaged. But does it matter? Let everyone say what
>*appears* to him to be the truth and leave *truth itself*
>to God!

We can also recall a passage quoted earlier[156] that goes in the
same direction: "It is mere pity that I cannot think without a pen
in my hand! I only think for my own instruction. If my thoughts
please me in the end I tear the paper to pieces. If they do not
please me I publish them." - In the light of such statements
ultimate significance should not be attributed to *The Education*.

A serious attempt link *The Education* with the Spinoza
conversations was recently made by H. Timm[157] in order to identify
the central text in Lessing. From the vantage point of *The
Education* Timm is able to present a unified, even systematic
interpretation of Lessing's work. Not only is *The Education* put at
the centre of Lessing's thought; but it is also read in the light of
the "Spinozism" of the conversations. This leads Timm to debate the
question of Lessing's Spinozism in the context of the Spinoza
renaissance of the 1780s. For him the real question is: What is that
"Spinozism" which contributed posthumously to make Lessing into
the prospective thinker of the following decades?[158] Timm's
investigation is then devoted to the articulation of "that Spinozism"
which he finds best expressed in *The Education* when read in the
light of the Spinoza conversations: "Only the conversation of
Wolfenbüttel can decipher the hermetic 100 §§ of *The Education of
the Human Race* and thereby uncover the systematic point of unity
of Lessing's entire thought."[159] The kind of Spinozism encountered
in Lessing is variously called: "reversed Spinozism"[160] that reads

---

[156] *Werke* VIII, p. 549.

[157] H. Timm, *Gott und die Freiheit*. 1974. Timm deals with Lessing throughout his book,
but more specifically in its first section [pp. 15-135].

[158] Timm, *Gott und die Freiheit*, p. 19.

[159] Timm, *Gott und die Freiheit*, pp. 38-39.

[160] Timm, *Gott und die Freiheit*, p. 136.

Spinoza's *Ethik* backwards and starts with the motif of love before moving to knowledge; that equates God-nature with Ego, and Subtance with subject; it is also called "heilsgeschichtlicher" Spinozism[161] because it introduces the idea of development into the *Ethik*; more often it is called "Christian Spinozism."[162] It is close to the "Weimar Spinozism"[163] of which Jacobi was prompt to say that it was pseudo-Christian.[164] Timm argues that Lessing "reorganized" Spinoza by bringing mysticism and rationalism again into a fruitful connection.[165] Once delineated, "that" Spinozism is resolutely used by Timm as "Interpretament"[166] for the understanding of *The Education* and thereby, in his view, of the entire work of Lessing.

The fascinating quality of Timm's investigation comes from the mastery with which it makes the philosophical debate of the years 1780-1790 genetically understandable. The concrete interaction of great thinkers is brought into the analysis to render the positions lively and likely. When we limit ourselves to the interpretation of Lessing found here, though, it leaves the clear impression of being forced. In spite of Timm's intention to steer between Jacobi's speculative straining [Konsequenzerei] and lack of humour, and Mendelssohn's minimizing of disturbing metaphors in their respective relation to the late Lessing, the decision to place *The Education* at the centre of a "systematic integration" of Lessing's efforts in the philosophy of religion predisposes the author to overlook essential features of the character of this ever-moving and fragmentary thinker. To be sure, Timm shows steady concern for linking the ideas of *The Education* with Lessing's intellectual biography and his self-interpretation in the Fragments controversy; and he might be right in viewing Lessing as a good mirror of all contemporary tendencies. But in the end Timm's Lessing remains, unfortunately, somewhat abstract. He is too much viewed as a systematic thinker who knew very well "from the beginning" what he was after, and who set out to unfold his system step by step,

---

[161] Timm, *Gott und die Freiheit*, p. 272.

[162] Timm, *Gott und die Freiheit*, pp. 193, 252, etc.

[163] Timm, *Gott und die Freiheit*, pp. 281-339.

[164] Timm, *Gott und die Freiheit*, p. 309.

[165] Timm, *Gott und die Freiheit*, p. 56.

[166] Timm, *Gott und die Freiheit*, p. 454.

always on edge to find a "mediation" between Christianity and modernity,[167] feeling and thinking, heart and head. The image of Lessing thus conveyed is one of an over-reflexive Lessing with a conscious and intentional biography, equal to a specialized philosopher and theologian with a well-defined programme. Timm's study confronts us with a skillful montage that fits the fragmentary utterances into the "final" Lessing and does not shrink from complementing the fragmentary Lessing: Timm bridges all the gaps in Lessing's thinking, not hesitating to take ideal associations for actual relations in order to make of Lessing a perfectly coherent thinker who always knew where he was heading. At many points Timm warns against the temptation of "over-interpretation"[168] to which those who attempt to overcome the stagnation of research are expposed. I think that he does not entirely resist the temptation.

When dealing specifically with the interpretation of the Spinoza conversations I recognize the value of connecting them with the views expressed in *The Education*. But when followed methodically, this procedure leads Timm to take every word of the conversations, even the less serious ones, at face value; Lessing's utterances are seen as the final, deliberate statements of a systematic position. Not only a full-fledged "Christian Spinozism" is read into *The Education*, the assumed sum of Lessing's life-work; but also the same fully developed position is read into the conversations. That is indeed too much "reading into." Timm is right in emphasizing the importance of Lessing's philosophical legacy, as formulated in *The Education* and in the Spinoza conversations, for the years to come. He goes beyond the evidence, though, when he assumes the dyad, *Education* / conversations, to be the unquestionable key-element in the interpret-ation of Lessing's entire work. Thereby the "character" of Lessing, as well as the specificity of his literary production, is overtly neglected. I wish therefore to look elsewhere for a more adequate hermeneutical orientation, convinced that numerous insights and perspectives presented by Timm can be made fruitful within a different framework.

---

[167] Timm, *Gott und die Freiheit*, pp. 120 and 145.

[168] Timm, *Gott und die Freiheit*, pp. 230 and 280 for instance.

The most likely candidate to be the key-text for the interpretation of Lessing is, according to me, *Nathan the Wise*. The late date of this play and its actual content are not the main reasons for considering it as such a central text. It is rather its form that makes it encapsulate best the style of Lessing's thought. The centrality of *Nathan* is suggested by Lessing's own famous words to E. Reimarus[169] explaining his return to the theatre as literary form: "I must try and see whether people will let me preach still undisturbed from my old pulpit, from the stage at least." Lessing's dramas represent not only so many critical exposures of prevailing ideologies, including the rationalist ideology;[170] by their very nature they embody a dialogical element attuned to Lessing's way of thinking. In his dramas Lessing's opinions and "positions" are, as it were, distributed among different roles and tried in a living contest. The dialectical elements of the theatrical scene, which continuously attracted Lessing, offer the interpretative key to his entire work: they were extended and transferred by him, now to the philosophical scene, now to the theological scene. Thus the theological controversy with Reß, Goeze, et al., in which metaphors from the stage play an important role, is itself viewed as a whole by Lessing in terms of the theatre: "I am particularly glad," he writes to his brother, "that you begin to enjoy the *haut-comique* of the polemic, which makes all other theatrical projects so insipid and wishy-washy."[171] Goeze did not miss the occasion to attack his opponent's "Theaterlogik,"[172] which gave Lessing the opportunity to explain his dialogical and metaphorical style[173] and to emphasize that his style does not follow any other "logic" than the only logic.[174] His activity as a

---

[169] Letter of September 6, 1778, *Werke* II, p. 719.

[170] See K.S. Guthke, *Lessing*. Stuttgart 1979, p. 95.

[171] Letter of February 25, 1778, *Werke* VIII, 607.

[172] In *Werke* VIII, pp. 170, 215, 268, 275, 289, 326, 329, 333-334.

[173] *Werke* VIII, pp. 194-196, 251-252, 603.

[174] *Werke* VIII, p. 195.

H. Timm, "Eine theologische Tragikomödie. Lessings Neu-inszenierung der Geistesgeschichte", *Zeitschrift für Religions- und Geistesgeschichte* 34[1982] 1-17 has recently drawn attention to the importance of the theatrical metaphor in Lessing's controversy with Goeze [p. 5: "ein Lustspiel größeren Formates"] as well as in his entire literary activity while in Wolfenbüttel [1770-1781] ["Wolfenbüttler Dramaturgie," Timm calls it].

publisher, for its part, can be likened to that of a stage director and his many "rescuings" finally manifest a dialectical quality which is not foreign to his dramatic vision.[175]

Should the Spinoza conversations themselves, viewed in that light, be interpreted as a theatrical dialogue? It does seem so. This is not meant to play down their importance or seriousness. On the contrary. All of Lessing's productions show the mark of the theatrical element and of its dialectical quality. It is only logical to apply this hermeneutical key to the Spinoza conversations as well.

---

[175] The interpretation of Lessing within such an aesthetic, instead of metaphysical framework is exemplified by the forthcoming work of Renate Homann.

TEXTS

from the pantheism debate between M. Mendelssohn and F.H. Jacobi, occasioned by Jacobi's report concerning Lessing's Spinozist leanings.

M. Mendelssohn, *Morgenstunden oder Vorlesungen über das Daseyn Gottes*. Berlin 1785.

[From H. Scholz, *Hauptschriften zum Pantheismusstreit zwischen Jacobi und Mendelssohn*. Berlin 1916, pp. 28-29, 29-44.]

[My translation of sections from Mendelssohn's two works is based on Scholz' text; I have also made use of the "Jubiläumsausgabe": Moses Mendelssohn, *Gesammelte Schriften* III,2 "Schriften zur Philosophie und Ästhetik" (Leo Strauss, ed.). Stuttgart - Bad Cannstadt 1974. My own additions are indicated by [= ...].]

From Lecture XIV

(...)

I, a human being, am a thought of the Divinity and never will I cease being a thought of the Divinity. In the endless course of the ages I will be blessed or wretched to the extent and degree of my recognition and love of him who is thinking me, depending on whether I strive (for Spinoza must allow even this thought of God the capacity to strive), depending on the degree to which I strive to resemble the source of my existence, strive to love all the other thoughts of his as much as I do myself. If my friend [= Lessing], that champion of a refined Spinozism, concedes all this (as he surely, in view of his principles, would have done), then morality and religion are in no danger; for, after all, this position is distinguished from our system only by a degree of subtlety which has no practical consequence, by an idle speculation as to whether God caused the thought of the best contingent world to radiate, to emanate, to pour forth - or what metaphor shall I use? (for the subtlety can scarcely be expressed save through metaphors); whether he caused the light to shine forth from him, or simply to gleam within himself; whether the source remained a spring, or whether it became a wellspring which poured itself forth into an everflowing flood. If we wish to visualize the processes of generating, creating, actualizing, etc. with the aid of such figurative expressions, then it is difficult to prevent a misinterpretation or misunderstanding from extending the metaphor beyond its limits and from leading us astray even to the point of atheism or religious madness [Schwärmerey], depending on whether one's temperament usually inclines to rapture or dry reflection. The corollaries of the two systems still seem to be far apart, which is basically due to a misinterpretation of one and the same metaphor: at times God is placed too figuratively in the world; at times the world is placed too figuratively in God. Sincere love for the truth soon leads us back to our point of departure and shows that we have simply become entangled in words. Do without words, friend of wisdom, and embrace thy brother!

Lecture XV

Lessing: His Contributions to the Religion of Reason; His Thoughts on Refined Pantheism

Our friend D., having paid us an unexpected visit during the last *Morgenstunde*, reproached me as he was leaving: "Where did you ever get the notion of making our Lessing the champion of such a misguided, ill-famed system [= Spinozist pantheism]? Was there no one else to whom you could entrust this questionable business?"

"You know," I answered, "it is *Lessing's* name which always comes to mind first if I am looking for an arbiter in such matters. I pursued philosophical discourse with him for quite some time; for years we exchanged views on such topics, with an ingenuous love of truth, which precluded dogmatism as well as false deference. It is only natural then that Lessing -- at times it may be mere habit -- should come to mind whenever a philosophical proposition is being mooted, whenever arguments and counter-arguments are to be weighed and compared."

"Yet I would hesitate," he said, "to make use of his name in this matter. I would not for the world wish to raise the slightest suspicion concerning the religious principles of this most excellent man. What, then? Lessing, a champion of pantheism, of a doctrine built upon the craftiest of sophistic foundations? a doctrine which, if it does not exactly subvert all the truths of natural religion, makes them at the very least extremely problematic? To whom but to him, the defender of the Fragmentist [= H.S. Reimarus], should the truths of the religion of reason be more inviolable? To the author of *Nathan*? There is no philosopher in Germany who has ever professed the religion of reason with more integrity, without admixture of error or prejudice, who has presented it to plain human understanding with stronger conviction than the Fragmentist. His devotion to natural religion was so great that in his zeal he would allow no revealed religion to stand beside it. He felt he had to extinguish all other light in order to let complete illumination flow forth from the light of reason in a single stream. With his defence of the Fragmentist, Lessing seems to have assumed also the full measure of his vision. Certainly, it is evident even in his earliest writings that, for him, the reasonable truths of religion and morality were ever holy and inviolable; but after Lessing's encounter with the Fragmentist, one can detect in his writings, in all the essays written in defence of his friend or "guest," as he calls him, the same quiet conviction so typical of the Fragmentist, the same ingenuous absence of morbid doubt, the same straight course of sound human reason where the truths of the religion of reason are concerned.

"And what of his *Nathan*? As far as certain truths of natural religion are concerned, I would venture to say of Lessing's masterpiece what Horace said of Homer in regard to morality:

> Qui, quid sit pulcrum, quid turpe, quid utile, quid non, planius ac melius Chrysippo et Crantore dicit.
> [= That poet shows what is fine and foul, what advisable and what is not, more clearly and better than Chrysippus and Crantor.] Horace, *Epist.* I.2.1-4

Especially concerning the doctrine of God's providence and governance, I know of no author who might have commended those glorious truths to the reader with the same degree of purity, the same power of conviction and concern as he.

> Cur ita crediderim, nisi quid te detinet, audi!
> [= I am happy to give you my reasons; hear them, if you are free to.] Horace, *Epist.* I.2.5

"In all observable human actions we notice a kind of opposition between majesty and humility, or between dignified reserve and intimacy, which clearly demonstrates the difficulty of finding these two moral qualities combined in one and the same person. Language itself confronts us with this contrast as we compare the derived moral sense of the words with their original concrete sense, and when we oppose majesty or excellence to humility. When something physically elevated is humbled, it ceases to be elevated. In the moral sphere as well, then, one is inclined to assume the impossibility of such a pairing, although here, in fact, precisely the opposite obtains; for the greatest moral excellence does consist in humbling oneself, and dignity without intimacy mistakes its true value. It is no small refinement of our concepts to be able, without falling prey to common prejudice, to perceive this difference between the moral and the physical. We know the story of that famous monarch who, while riding a cock-horse around a table with his children, was interrupted by the arrival of a foreign ambassador. The king asked him, and properly so: "Are you married?" "Yes," was the answer. "Do you have children?" "Yes." "Well then, in you come," were the words of this most excellent king; he could credit only a father with having the good sense to know that his dignity loses nothing if he stoop to the level of a child. A truth such as this is rarely recognized by a courtier bereft of all feeling. For such a person, humbling oneself usually amounts to pusillanimity; a father's warmth, to little more than weakness.

"As regards religion, the same difficulty inherent in pairing these two qualities has from time immemorial led the human race down the garden path, but in diametrically opposed directions; either the majesty or the condescension of the divine being was exaggerated: at times he was excluded from all co-operation, at times made so much a part of human endeavour that he of necessity partook of human frailty. Those philosophers who did understand what God's infinity means thought it unworthy of him to be concerned with the destiny of humans and of other finite beings. They therefore exalted their Divinity totally above and beyond this sub-lunar world and entrusted it with the sole task of preserving the whole, with the care of the species and genera of things, in total disregard of the vicissitudes and experiences of individual beings, be they rational or irrational in nature. The popular view proposed by poets and priests was the exact opposite. Not only did they ascribe to the direct intervention of their divinities all cataclysmic changes and events, political revolutions, wars and devastations; they would even bring their Jupiters home as house guests to their Philemons and Baucises and have them share, as courteous guests, the humble lot of these lowly countryfolk. While on the one hand this type of popular understanding effectively brought the Divine closer, as it were, to humankind, making them at once witness to and judge of human actions and, further, comforters amid the tribulations of this life, it was on the other hand flawed by its debasing the divinity to the level of human frailty and by its failure to recognize fully the infinite sublimity and self-sufficiency of the Divine.

"In this popular doctrine, furthermore, the hand of the Divinity was evident only in extraordinary and spectacular cases or in wondrous works; that is, only in those particular occurrences in which a sense of purpose is obvious and where the influence of a Being endowed with free will, acting consciously and with intent, is beyond doubt. But as for the general course of things, where everything seems to follow fixed rules, it was considered to be the result of the operation of nature, to the total exclusion of any divine co-operation. The natural order and God's will were like polar opposites. The more one discovered order and regularity in the workings of nature, the less room was left for God's governance; that is why the first natural scientists were also the first atheists.

"You know," he continued, "that the greatest men of the last century had not yet managed to clarify those concepts entirely. They always gave preference to the philosophical prejudice that the highest cause acts solely in accordance with general laws. It was merely as an instance of the universal that the particular was the object of divine control. In itself, the particular could be in conformity with or in opposition to divine intention; following the general laws of nature it had to be permitted by divine governance, or else it had to be set aside by direct intervention, i.e., by a miracle.

"It is the singular triumph of human wisdom to recognize a most perfect harmony between the doctrine of intentions and that of efficient causes, to understand with Shaftesbury and Leibniz that God's intentions as well as his co-operation extend into the smallest transformations and particular occurrences of both inorganic matter and organic life; that two sets of laws arise from the similarity of individual things, events, and ultimate purposes: the general laws of intentions and, in complete accord with them, the general laws of efficient causes; that there is not a single lacuna, and that each natural effect agrees with divine intention, just as surely as it flows from his omnipotence. To me, it seems that the consummate refinement of human thought, the most sublime way of thinking about God, his governance and providence lies herein: to glorify God in natural occurrences rather that in miraculous ones; to recognize God's providence and governance in the minutest of occurrences, to appreciate them for the very reason that they develop in the normal course of nature."

I expressed my approval of his exposition and quoted the words of a rabbi who once noted the contrast between majesty and humility: "Where'er thou findest the majesty and sublimity of God, there also willst thou find Him humbling Himself." The scriptural passages with which this teacher, in true rabbinical style, substantiates this doctrine are especially remarkable, as is the lyrical turn given it by the Psalmist:

> Who is like unto the Lord our God?
> Who dwelleth on high?
> Who humbleth himself to behold the things
> that are in heaven
> or in earth? [= Ps 113: 5-6]

D. continued: "Now, my friend, it seems to me that no author has propounded this very doctrine with more conviction and accuracy of detail, with more fervent passion and pious enthusiasm than our own immortal Lessing. We need but recall those superb scenes from his didactic drama [= *Nathan the Wise*] in which he presented most vividly the true doctrine of God's providence and governance along with the perniciousness of constantly searching for miracles in order to perceive the hand of God; we need but remember how he managed to do that with all the precision of the didactic philosopher and, at the same time, with all the vigour of the dramatic poet. A combination possible only in a Lessing, and perhaps even for him it was possible only in our own mother tongue. It is our mother tongue alone which seems to have achieved a stage of development which permits the liveliest manner of exposition to be conjoined with the language of reason itself."

"It seems to me," I said, "as if Lessing intended his *Nathan* as a kind of *Anti-Candide*. The French writer [= Voltaire] summoned all his power of wit, spurred on the inexhaustible humour of his satirical bent; in a word, he exerted all the extraordinary talents Providence had given him in order to satirize that selfsame Providence. The German writer [= Lessing] did the same thing to vindicate Providence, and did it with a view to presenting it to mortal eyes in its purest and most radiant form. I well remember that my late friend, soon after the appearance of *Candide*, did for a time entertain the thought of writing a play to counter it or, rather, to follow upon it; by means of a series of events he wished to show that all the evils Voltaire mustered and deployed dramatically in an attempt to vilify Providence would, nevertheless, ultimately turn out for the best and be found to be in complete accord with the intentions of the most highest wisdom. It seems that the French satirist rendered the task too difficult for him, having marshalled in poetic form more evils than a new poetic form could put to flight. And so Lessing preferred to go his own way, creating a sequence of events which do indeed, in point of wit and poetic force, bear comparison with *Candide* (don't you agree?), and which, in its high seriousness of purpose, its wisdom and usefulness, stands in about the same relation to *Candide* as does heaven to hell or as do the ways of the Tempter to the ways of God."

"It was precisely this glorious paean in praise of Providence," D. rejoined, "this felicitous attempt at justifying God's ways to man that cost our immortal friend so dearly! Alas! it embittered his last days and may well have shortened his life that was so dear to us. As he was editing the *Fragments* he fully anticipated the attack of that whole pack of writers, properly qualified or no, whose intent it would be to refute the *Fragments*; and he considered himself strong enough to defend his guest against all the loutish assaults of his opponents. Varied as were the routes his adversaries could take and, as events showed, did indeed take in order to assail him, he still thought he could hold his own against those who exhibited neither decency nor love of truth. No matter how spiritedly he conducted the controversy, it remained, in the end, a purely academic quarrel that was to cause each side many disagreeable and agreeable moments; but in his opinion it was not to have any substantial effect on human happiness. Yet how the scene changed with the appearance of *Nathan*! Intrigue now rushed out of the scholar's cloistered study and the bookstore, breaking into the very homes of his friends and acquaintances, putting it into everyone's ear: Lessing has vilified *Christianity* - even though it had only ventured to utter a few reproaches against some individual Christians and, at the worst, against *Christendom*. Actually we must admit that his *Nathan* truly redounds to the honour of Christianity. The degree of enlightenment and education attained by a nation must be high indeed if one of its citizens can soar to such sublimity of mind and develop such an excellent knowledge of things human and divine. Though Lessing's contemporaries did not think so, posterity at least will, I warrant, be of this opinion. Any reproach of personal conceit or prejudice which he directed at some of his co-religionists or expressed in his dramatic characters was taken by one and all as a personal affront. Lessing, who had been welcomed everywhere as a friend and acquaintance, now met on every side with blank faces, reserved or frosty stares, cool greetings and all too eager farewells; he saw himself abandoned by friends and acquaintances and exposed to the snares of his persecutors. How strange! Even among the most gullible of the French, *Candide* had for Voltaire nowhere near the same dire consequences; his libelling of Providence aroused nowhere near the same hostility Lessing incurred from the most enlightened of the Germans when he defended that same Providence in his *Nathan*. Sad indeed were the effects upon his spirit. Lessing, who despite all scholarly preoccupations had always proved the most pleasant of companions, the most convivial of guests at table, now lost all his joviality and turned into a torpid and insensate automaton."

"Stay, my friend," I interrupted him. "Spare me this gloomy memory."

"Let be then," he said. "This melancholy recollection is a bleak one and is in no way appropriate to my present purpose. I wished only to mention what Lessing had done and suffered on behalf of the truth of the religion of reason and how deserving he was of its friends and adherents. He is much too much a man of honour to be misused in the defense of error. If you want your friend to be party still to your philosophical discussions, at least impute to him no worse an opinion than he himself espoused. Do not make him into the champion of a false doctrine from which he was, perforce, so very distant."

"Then you do think that Lessing," said I, "in keeping with his character, would have been pleased to see me demolish pantheism or Spinozism whether I did this for good or bad reasons?"

"Well, perhaps he would not go that far."

"That would be completely out of keeping with his character which would make him more likely to defend any persecuted doctrine, whether he inclined to it or not, and to muster all his acumen in order to add something to its justification. If somebody propounded even the most erroneous statement, the most absurd opinion with shallow arguments, you can rest assured that Lessing would have come to its defence. The spirit of inquiry was everything to him. He used to say that a truth asserted with shallow reasoning is prejudice no less harmful than obvious error, at times even more harmful; for such a prejudice deadens the desire for further research and kills the spirit of inquiry. Had the critics of the *Fragments* defended them with bad arguments, I am convinced that Lessing would have been the first to challenge them."

"I heard with sincere delight," I continued, "the praise of our friend coming from your lips. Ah! amidst the indifference or ingratitude of the many, it is comforting, most comforting, to see the memory of such benefactors preserved so fresh in noble minds, to see it bearing fruit. I commend also the zeal with which you adopt the religious principles of this philosopher. I wholeheartedly acknowledge the sincerity and honesty of his sentiments whenever the most important truths of religion are discussed, yet I do not deem it necessary to beg his spirit's forgiveness for enrolling him in the defence of pantheism. As I knew him, he was able to defend even an error with zeal, without himself being partial toward it, when the reasons invoked for its refutation were not sufficient.

"In the course of my previous lecture I also showed that refined pantheism is totally compatible with the truths of religion and morality, that the difference resides merely in an overly subtle speculation which, far from influencing human actions and happiness in the least, instead leaves open what can result in practice and what can be of noticeable consequence in the life, or even in the thought, of human beings.

"Here is a passage from a posthumous theological work of Lessing [= published in 1784 by Lessing's brother] that will convince you of the fact that he thought as I claim on this point. True, it comes, as I recall, from a very early essay, the essence of which he read to me at the very beginning of our relationship. Yet it at least demonstrates for you the turn which, even so early on, he was able to give to such a speculation; and if I read correctly, a short piece which he published just before his death [= *The*

Education of the Human Race (1780)] also bears obvious traces of the same way of thinking.

"The passage is taken from the twelfth essay of his posthumous work entitled *The Christianity of Reason* [= written in 1751/52]. I shall quote for you its most important propositions, for it consists entirely of separate statements which were found as drafts among his papers. They are as follows:

§ 1

The one most perfect Being has been able from all eternity to be concerned with nothing but the consideration of that which is most perfect.

§ 2

That which is most perfect is he himself; and thus, from all eternity, God has been able to think only himself.

§ 3

With God, to conceive [vorstellen], to will, and to create are one. One can therefore say that everything which God conceives, he also creates.

§ 4

God can think himself in only two ways: either he thinks all his perfections at once, and himself as the sum and substance of them all, or he thinks his perfections individually, one separated from another, and each one divided in itself by degrees.

§ 5

From all eternity God thought himself in all his perfection; that is, from all eternity God created for himself a being lacking no perfection which he himself possessed.

"In Lessing's subsequent propositions, by a not inelegant development, he attempts to explain the mystery of the Trinity; or, as he often flattered himself in his earlier years, he goes so far as to try to demonstrate it metaphysically. To be sure, he later abandoned such youthful pretentions, with which the strictest adherents of the Athanasian doctrine themselves are not satisfied.

Yet, it is here that we can still recognize the clearest traces of that kind of speculation which for me is proof that the essay must be from an early date. Lessing continues:

§ 13
God thought his perfections separately; that is, he created beings, each one of which has something of his perfections; for, I reiterate, with God, every thought is a creation.

§ 14
All these beings together are called the world.

§ 15
God might think of his perfections as divided in an infinite variety of ways. There might therefore be an infinite number of possible worlds were not God always to think the most perfect; and thus amongst all these ways, to have thought the most perfect way and, in so doing, to have made it real.

§ 16
The most perfect way of thinking his perfections separately is to think them separately on an infinite scale of greater or less, which so follow upon one another that there is never a break or a gap between them.

§ 17
Therefore, the beings in this world must be ordered according to such a scale. They must form a series in which each member contains everything which the lower members have, together with something more; but this something more never reaches the final limit.

§ 18
Such a series must be an infinite series, and in this sense the infinity of the world is incontrovertible.

§ 19
God creates nothing but simple beings, and the complex is nothing but a consequence of his creation.

§ 20
Since each of these simple beings has something which the others have, and none can have anything which the others do not have, there must exist a harmony among these simple beings; and from this harmony everything may be explained that happens among them, that is, in the world.

§ 21
One day, some fortunate Christian will extend the sphere of natural philosophy to this point, but only after long centuries when explanations will have been found for all phenomena in nature so that there is nothing left to do except trace them to their true origin.

§ 22
Since these simple beings are, as it were, limited gods, even their perfections must be similar to the perfections of God, just as parts are similar to the whole.

§ 23
To God's perfections belong both the consciousness of his perfection and the power to act according to his perfection. Both are, as it were, the seal of his perfections.

§ 24
It follows that, to the various grades of his perfection there must be connected various degrees of the consciousness of these perfections and of the power to act in accordance with them.

§ 25
Beings endowed with perfections, with the consciousness of their perfections, and with the power to act in accordance with them, are called *moral beings*, that is, beings which can follow a law.

§ 26
This law is derived from their own nature and can be none other than this: *act according to your own individual perfections*.

§ 27
Since there cannot possibly be a break in the series of beings, beings must also exist which are not conscious of their perfections with sufficient clarity....

"You see," I added in conclusion, "that Lessing envisaged pantheism in the totally refined manner I have ascribed to him: in complete harmony with whatever has a bearing on life and happiness; indeed, that he was on his way to link pantheistic concepts even with positive religion. This linking is in fact as possible with pantheism as with the Ancients' system of emanation which, throughout the centuries, was accepted by religion and held to be the only orthodox doctrine. On the long road which takes one from these overly subtle speculations to the praxis of religion and morality, there are many points where one can effortlessly re-enter the open highway from a by-way. Just as an error in calculation can be cancelled out and corrected through another error, one inaccuracy in such abstract meditations can quickly be corrected by another, or one small digression which might, in the event, have led us far from our goal can be rectified by an equally small turn, and we are back on the road. Hence the contemptibility of excessive consistency which from time immemorial has spawned, or at least nourished, all the persecutions and religious hatred of the human race.

F.H. Jacobi, *Über die Lehre des Spinoza, in Briefen an den Herrn Moses Mendelssohn*. Breslau 1785[1], 1789[2]; *Werke* IV, 1-2, Leipzig 1819.

[From Scholz, *Hauptschriften*, pp. 65-122, 137-140, 165-173, 180-183.]

[My translation of passages from Jacobi's two books follows the last edition of his works in 1819 as given by Scholz. Significant changes from the first edition are indicated in the *numbered* footnotes, following Scholz. The numerous and, at times, extensive footnotes added by Jacobi himself are translated only when they contain elements essential for interpreting the conversations between Lessing and Jacobi; they are then indicated by *asterisks*. My own editorial explanations are indicated by [= ...]. Wherever Jacobi uses the pseudonym "Emilie," I have replaced it by "Elise (Reimarus)."]

Dos moi pou sto [= Give me where to stand and I will move the earth. Archimedes]

An intimate friend of Lessing [= Elise Reimarus], who through him became mine as well, wrote to me in February 1783 that she was about to go on a journey to Berlin and asked me whether I had any messages to deliver.

From Berlin my friend wrote me again. Her letter dealt mainly with Mendelssohn, "that true admirer and friend of our Lessing." She informed me that she had spoken at length with Mendelssohn about our recently deceased friend and also about myself; and that Mendelssohn was at last about to embark upon his long-promised work on Lessing's character and writings.

Various complications made it impossible for me to answer that letter immediately, and my friend's stay in Berlin was to last only a few weeks.

Once she was home again, I wrote her to enquire how much or how little Mendelssohn was familiar with Lessing's religious views. I mentioned that *Lessing was a Spinozist.*[*]

---

[*] Here is the passage from my letter to Elise (July 21, 1783) without a single syllable changed:

"... I was not able to answer your letter by return post because I wanted to tell you something of great importance: about our Lessing's thinking toward the end of his life, and that Mendelssohn might be so instructed, should you find it appropriate. - You know perhaps, and if you do not know, I confide it to you here *sub rosa*, that Lessing was in his final days a firm [entschiedener] Spinozist. It is conceivable that Lessing may have expressed this view to others; in that case, it would be necessary for Mendelssohn, in the memorial he intends to dedicate to him, either to avoid certain matters totally or at least to treat them with the utmost caution. Perhaps Lessing expressed himself to his dear Mendelssohn as clearly as he did to me; or again, perhaps not -- because he had not conversed with him for a long time and wrote letters only with reluctance. It is a matter for your discretion, my dear and trusted friend, whether or not you wish to disclose any of this to Mendelssohn; but for now I can write in no greater detail."

Lessing had expressed himself to me personally on that topic without the slightest reserve; since he was not by nature inclined to conceal his opinions, I had good reason to assume that what I heard from him was known to many. But that he had never declared himself clearly on that matter to Mendelssohn, I discovered as follows.

In 1779, having promised Lessing a visit the following Summer, I notified him in a letter dated June 1st, 1780, of my impending arrival and at the same time invited him to accompany me afterwards on a journey which would take us to Berlin. In reply, Lessing answered that we would discuss my proposed journey in Wolfenbüttel. On my arrival, serious difficulties arose. Lessing urged me to travel to Berlin without him and pressed me the more as the days passed. His chief reason was the thought of Mendelssohn, whom he esteemed most among his friends. It was his avid wish that I make his personal acquaintance. In one of our conversations I expressed my astonishment that a man of such clear and sure understanding as Mendelssohn could have assumed the proof of God's existence from its idea [= the ontological argument] with the fervour he showed in his treatise on evidence [= *Concerning Evidence in the Metaphysical Sciences* (1763), which contains Mendelssohn's formulation of the ontological argument]. Lessing's apologies led me directly to ask whether he had ever propounded his own system to Mendelssohn. "Never," Lessing answered.... "But once I did speak to him about approximately the same things that caught your attention in my *Education of the Human Race* (§73). We could not reach any agreement and I left it at that."

The probability then, on the one hand, that many knew of Lessing's Spinozism and on the other, the certainty that Mendelssohn had heard nothing definite about it, moved me to drop him a hint.

My friend Elise understood my point perfectly well. The matter appeared to her to be of extreme importance and she wrote Mendelssohn post haste in order to let him know what I had just disclosed to her.

I will quote here in its entirety the answer I then received from Elise.

Hamburg, September 1, 1783

"I wanted to wait for Mendelssohn's answer, my dear Jacobi, before writing you again. It has now arrived.

"Mendelssohn wishes[1] to know exactly how Lessing expressed the views in question. Whether he came right out and said: I consider Spinoza's system to be true and well founded? And which system did he mean? the one put forward in the *Tractatus theologico-politicus* or the one in *De principiis philosophiae cartesianae*; or the one that Ludovicus Mayer circulated under Spinoza's name after his death? If he was referring to the system of Spinoza generally known as the *atheistic* one, he asks further, whether Lessing understood it with the mis-understanding of a Bayle or with the better understanding of some others? He adds: If Lessing was capable of declaring himself, so baldly and without any qualification, for the system of just any individual, then he was at that time no longer himself or he was in one of his fanciful moods where he was asserting something paradoxical which, in a more serious moment, he would reject.

"But if," Mendelssohn continues, "what he perhaps said was: My dear fellow, the greatly maligned Spinoza may in many respects have had a clearer vision than all the loud mouths who became heroes merely by attacking him; his *Ethics* in particular contains excellent things, perhaps better than can be found in many an orthodox moral treatise or philosophical compendium; his system makes more sense than is generally believed. - Well, then: Mendelssohn can surely live with that.

"He concludes with the wish that you be so kind as to relay to him detailed information as to the following: what, how, and on what occasion did Lessing express himself on this issue? For Mendelssohn is firmly convinced that you understood Lessing fully, and that your memory will have retained every detail of so important an exchange.

---

[1] The first edition has: "Mendelssohn was astonished, and his first reaction was to doubt the accuracy of my assertion. He wished etc."

"Once this is done, Mendelssohn will of course make mention of this matter in whatever he still intends to write concerning Lessing's character. For, he says, the name of even our best friend must shine for posterity no more brightly than it truly deserves. Truth stands only to gain from this. If his reasons are superficial, they will aid the final triumph of truth; if they are a threat, then *la belle dame* can look to her own defence. All in all, he adds, when I write on Lessing's character, I project myself half a century ahead, when partisanship will have ceased to be and all our present vexations been forgotten.

"You see, dearest Jacobi, here is the result of your communication; I could not really keep it from Mendelssohn but you should not hesitate to add to it. For what would you say if one day Mendelssohn were to come forward with what he has to say about Lessing's character and no mention were to be made there of similar important issues? Then you would have to reproach yourself for having crippled the cause of truth (for in the last analysis it is less our friend's cause than the cause of truth). Otherwise, it matters not how I might feel, however you may decide to reply...."

I did not hesitate for a moment to meet this challenge and on November 4th I dispatched, in an envelope addressed to my lady friend, the following unsealed letter to Mendelssohn!* To retain the

---

* With the letter I enclosed the following for Elise:

November 4, 1783

... The enclosed is something which, to my own regret, I have owed you for so long. Do not be offended that my letter is addressed directly to Mendelssohn; and Mendelssohn shall not take offence that it is not completely in my own hand. I leave it to you to express my apologies to him for all this.

If you can, let me know by Monday's post, that you have received and forwarded the packet, and also what you think of its content. Let me hear later as much as I may know of what Mendelssohn has to say to it. I hardly expect his warmest gratitude for my pains since my way of looking at things is somewhat different from his.... But I am totally resigned to bearing whatever the consequences may be of how I appear to others [aus dem Scheine meines Seyns] and resigned always to presenting my Self as I

letter's documentary nature, I shall reproduce it, unaltered, from the first word to the last.[1]

Pempelfort near Düsseldorf, November 4, 1783

You wish me to tell you in greater detail about certain opinions which I, in a letter to Elise Reimarus, attributed to our late friend Lessing; so it would seem best to address you directly with what I am able to relate of these opinions.

It is relevant to the issue, or at least to its presentation, that I preface it with a few remarks concerning myself. And by allowing you to know me better, I shall muster the courage necessary to express myself frankly and even to disregard what would otherwise tend to make me timid or cautious.

I was still but a child when I began to worry about things of an other world. Childlike pensiveness led me at the age of seven or eight to certain singular notions (I do not know what else to call them) to which I have held fast ever since. My longing for certainty as regards higher human aspirations grew with each passing year and became the dominant theme to which all the eventualities of my subsequent life would perforce relate. My inherent disposition and my education joined to keep alive in me a proper scepticism toward myself and, for too long a time, a proportionally greater belief in the achievement of others. I came to Geneva where I found most excellent men who lavished on me generous love and genuine fatherly devotion. Later acquaintances of equal reputation, many of an even greater one, failed to offer me the advantages I had enjoyed from my earlier ones; and I had to draw back from more than a few of the later acquaintances with regret and remorse for the lost time and wasted energy. These and other experiences turned me little by little back upon myself; I learned to collect my true strengths and take counsel with them.

---

am. This requires some measure of courage and self-denial, but as a compensation one does gain an otherwise unobtainable inner peace.

[1] This solemn claim to documentary accuracy is a rhetorical phrase typical of Jacobi. Only the sense remains the same; the text is different in all three editions. In the following we refer only to textual alterations relating to the conversation with Lessing. (Scholz)

It is a fact that every age has seen but a few people who strove after truth with any real intensity; it is also a fact that truth, for its part, revealed itself in some manner or other to those few. I hit upon this path; I traced it in the works of the living and the dead. And the longer I followed the trail, the more intimately I became aware that all genuine profundity leads in one single direction, just as the force of gravity works on physical bodies; but, to use an analogy, that direction, since it has its origin at various points on a perimeter, can no more yield parallel lines than it can lines which intersect. Acumen is quite a different matter: it is often confused with profundity because it expresses itself in a profound manner about relationships and form. Acumen I would compare to the chords of an arc; there, lines intersect wherever one wants and sometimes even run parallel. The chord of an arc can be drawn so close to a diameter that it may be taken for the diameter itself; but it is simply cutting through a greater number of radii without ever ceasing to be a chord.

Please forgive me all this metaphoric by-play, most honoured sir. — I come to Lessing.

I had always admired the great man; but my desire to become better acquainted with him first quickened after his theological controversies and following my reading of his *Parable* [= published in March 1778]. It was my good fortune that he took interest in my *Allwill* [= *Eduard Allwills Papiere* (1775/76), a philosophical novel] and sent me many a friendly word, at first by people passing through, and then in 1779 in a letter. I responded that I was planning a journey for the following Spring which would take me through Wolfenbüttel, where through him I longed to conjure up the spirit of the many sages whom I could not get to respond to me on certain topics.

My journey was undertaken and on the afternoon of July 5th I embraced Lessing for the first time.

That day we talked about many important things; and also about individual persons, moral and immoral, atheists, theists[1], and Christians.

---

[1] The first edition has here and in the following: "deists."

The following morning I was still busy finishing several letters when Lessing came to my room. To help him pass the time I handed him some papers from my folder. Having finished them he asked whether I had more he might read. "Indeed I do!" I said, in the act of sealing my letters: "there is a poem in here too; you have so often given offence that you will not mind taking offence for once"*....

Lessing: (after reading the poem and returning it to me) I take no offence; I long ago became acquainted with it first hand.

I: You know the poem?

Lessing: I have never read the poem; but I find it good.

I: I find it good too, in its way; otherwise I would not have shown it to you.

Lessing: That's not what I mean.... The point of view in which the poem is cast is my own point of view.... The orthodox concepts of the divinity are no longer for me; I cannot stand them. *Hen kai Pan*! [= One and All] I know naught else. That is also the tendency in this poem; and I must admit, I like it very much.

I: Then you would indeed be more or less in agreement with Spinoza.

Lessing: If I am to call myself by anybody's name, then I know none better.

---

* Goethe's poem "Prometheus" (see *Introduction* above).

[= In consideration of sensitive souls or zealous censors Jacobi had the poem printed on two loose pages without page number; they could easily be removed and replaced by a note that said, among other things: "For good reasons, that poem, directed in very harsh words at providence itself, cannot be printed here."]

I: Spinoza is good enough for me; nevertheless there is scant benefit [schlechtes Heil] to be found in that name.

Lessing: Well fine, if that is what you think!... And yet... are you aware of a better one?

In the meantime, Director Wolke from Dessau had come in and together we went to the library.

The next morning when I had returned to my room to dress after breakfast, Lessing followed me in a little later. As soon as the servants had left he began:

Lessing   I came to talk with you about my *Hen kai Pan*. You looked startled yesterday.

I: You surprised me and[1] I felt confused. Dismay it was not. I certainly did not expect to find you a Spinozist or pantheist; and[2] still less did I expect that you would put it to me directly and so frankly and clearly. I had come chiefly in the hope of receiving your help against Spinoza.

Lessing: Then you really do know him?

I: I believe[3] as probably only very few have.

Lessing: Then there is no help for you. Why don't you become his friend openly? There is no other philosophy but the philosophy of Spinoza.

I: That may be true. For if a determinist wants to be consistent, he must become a fatalist; all else will follow as a matter of course.

Lessing: I can see we understand each other. That makes me the more eager to hear from you what you consider to be

---

[1] The first edition adds: "I probably turned from white to red; for..."

[2] The first edition has: "you put it to me so bluntly."

[3] The first edition has: "I believe hardly anybody has known him as well as I."

the *spirit* of Spinozism; I mean the spirit which possessed Spinoza himself.

I: Probably it was none other than is found in the time-honoured phrase *a nihilo nihil fit* [= nothing is made out of nothing] which Spinoza contemplated, applying more abstract concepts than did the philosophising Cabbalists and others before him. When using those more abstract concepts he found a *something out of nothing* to be posited by anything that originated within the infinite, no matter what metaphors or words one might use to express it[1], or by each and every change within the infinite. And so he rejected any *transition* from the infinite to the finite [= creation]; he rejected transient causes altogether, be they secondary or remote. In the place of the emanating One he posited an Ensoph that was *immanent* only: an inherent cause of the world, eternally unchangeable *in itself*, which, taken together with all that followed from it, would be One and the Same.

... *

The immanent infinite cause as such is explicitly devoid of both reason [Verstand] and will; for, as a consequence of its transcendental *unity* and constant absolute infinity, it cannot have any object of thinking and willing [des Denkens und des Wollens]; because it is absurd that a power bring forth a concept *before the concept* or that a concept precede its object and be *the complete cause of itself*, and absurd that a will effect willing and determine itself *completely*....

... The objection - that an infinite series of effects is impossible (these are not *mere* effects because the immanent cause is

---

[1] The first edition has: "with whatever metaphors one might cloak it."

* In the remainder of this presentation, for brevity's sake, I condense as much as I can by not recording the interruptions. What follows at this point was said as Lessing made mention of what he found most obscure in Spinoza, something which Leibniz also had felt and did not entirely understand (*Theodicy* § 173). This is the only time I will note this. In future when I take the liberty of condensing, I shall make no note of it.

everywhere and forever) - refutes itself because any series which is not to originate from *nothing* must of necessity be infinite. It follows from this (since every particular concept must spring from another particular concept and be *immediately* related to a *really existing object*) that the first cause, which is of infinite nature, contains neither particular ideas nor particular determinations of the will but merely their internal, initial, general prime matter [Urstoff].... The first cause can no more act according to intentions or ends than it can exist for the sake of a certain intention or final cause; it can no more have the *first motive* or *final goal* to perform something any more than it can have a *beginning* or an *end* .... But basically, what we call sequence or duration is mere illusion; for since the *real effect* is given, together with its *complete real* cause, and is distinct from it only in our minds [der Vorstellung nach], then sequence and duration must simply be *in truth* a certain manner of viewing the manifold within the infinite.

Lessing: Let us not quarrel over our credo.

I: Quarrel, certainly not. But my credo is not to be found in Spinoza.[1] *I believe in an intelligent personal first cause of the world.*

Lessing: Oh! all the better! Now I am going to hear something quite new.

I: Do not rejoice too soon. I extricate myself from the affair by a *salto mortale* and you do not usually take great pleasure in somersaults.

Lessing: Say not so; provided I am not required to follow suit. And anyway you will soon land back on your feet. If it is not a secret, I insist on hearing what you have to say.

I: You could always learn the trick from me. The whole

---

[1] The first and second editions add:
"Lessing: I sincerely hope that it is not to be found in any book.
I: That certainly not."

matter consists in my arguing from fatalism directly against fatalism and all that is connected with it.

If there are only efficient causes and no final ones, then the thinking faculty can, in all of nature, do nothing but observe; its sole function is to accompany the mechanism of efficient powers. The conversation we are now having is merely a concern of our bodies and the whole content of this conversation is reduced to its elements: extension, movement, degree of velocity, along with our concepts of them, and the concepts of those concepts. The inventor of the clock did not, strictly speaking, invent it; he only watched its formation out of the blindly evolving energies. Raphael did the same when he was sketching out the School of Athens as did Lessing when he was writing his *Nathan*. The same applies to all philosophies, arts, forms of government, wars at sea and on land: in short, to everything possible. For even affects and passions do not cause anything at all: they are merely perceptions and ideas; or better, they *come encumbered with* perceptions and ideas. We only *believe* that we act out of anger, love, magnanimity, or reasonable resolve. Pure illusion! Ultimately, what moves us in all those cases is a *Something* which *knows nothing* of all that and, *to that extent*, is totally bereft of sensation and idea. But sensation and idea are purely concepts of extension, movement, degrees of velocity etc. Now if anyone can accept such a view, I would not know how to refute his opinion. But if a person cannot accept it, he would have to be Spinoza's exact opposite.

Lessing: I notice that you would like very much to have your will free. I covet no free will. All in all, what you just said does not shock me in the least. Human prejudice has it that we consider the idea as primary and supreme, and want to derive everything from it since everything, including representations, is dependent upon higher principles. Extension, movement, idea are obviously grounded in a higher energy which is far from exhausting itself in them. It must be infinitely superior to one effect or the other; so it can even take a kind of pleasure which not only surpasses all concepts but also lies totally *outside* all concept. The fact that we cannot even think about this does not preclude its possibility.

I: You are going further than Spinoza. *Understanding* [Einsicht] was everything to him.

Lessing: Only as far as *human beings* are concerned! He was, however, far from considering as the best method our wretched way of acting according to intentions and of giving the idea pride of place.

I: For Spinoza, understanding is the best part in *all finite* natures because it is that part by virtue of which every finite nature extends beyond its finitude. You might even say that Spinoza himself attributed two souls to every being: one, related only to the present particular thing, and another, related to the whole. To his second soul he grants immortality as well. But as for Spinoza's infinite Unique Substance, it has of itself and aside from the particular things no proper or special[1] existence. If the Substance as One (if I may put it so) were to have proper, special, particular reality, i.e., personality and life, then understanding would also be its best part.

Lessing: Well and good. But what representations enable you to posit your personal, extra-mundane divinity? Could they perhaps be those of Leibniz? I am afraid, he was himself a Spinozist at heart.

I: Are you serious?

Lessing: Do you seriously doubt it? Leibniz' concepts of truth were so constituted that he could not bear it if it were set too narrow limits. Many of his assertions can be traced to that way of thinking; and even if we summon up our greatest acumen it is often very difficult to discover what he actually meant. This is precisely why I esteem him so highly. I mean to say: it was not because of any one of his opinions he seemed to hold or perhaps

---

[1] The first edition has: "definite or complete."

really did hold; it was because of the grand manner of his thinking.

I: Quite right. Leibniz really liked to "strike fire from every stone" [= see Lessing, "Leibniz on Eternal Punishments," *Werke* VII, 180]. But you said that Leibniz was "at heart devoted to" a certain philosophical position, Spinozism.

Lessing: Do you remember that passage in Leibniz where he says of God that he is in a perpetual state of expansion and contraction? [= in Lurianic Cabbala, the doctrine of Zimzum] which is the creation and continued existence of the world.

I: I am not familiar with that passage, though I know of his "fulgurations" [= created or derived monads that come into being through continuous flashing radiations of the divinity. See *Monadologie* § 47].

Lessing: I will look it up and then you will please tell me what a man like Leibniz was thinking or *must* have been thinking when he wrote it.

I: Show me the passage. But I can tell you right now that, in the light of so many other passages by that very Leibniz, in the light of so many of his letters, essays, of his *Theodicy* and *Nouveaux Essais*, of his whole philosophical development, I am made dizzy by the mere hypothesis that such a man is supposed to have posited just an Intra-mundane first cause of the world rather than a Supra-mundane one.

Lessing: If you approach it from that direction, then I must yield. That approach will remain the definitive one and I admit that I went a bit too far. Nevertheless, the passage I am talking about - as well as some others - is most striking. --- But there is something else we must keep in mind. How on earth can you believe the opposite of Spinozism? Do you find Leibniz' *Principia* [= *Principes de la nature et de la grâce fondés en raison*] put an end to Spinozism?

I: How could I, since I am firmly convinced that a
consistent determinist is no different from a fatalist?...
The monads with their *vincula* [= hooks] make extension
and thinking - indeed, *reality* in general - no more
comprehensible to me than ever they were before; and I
don't know where to turn....[1] For I still know of no
other system that agrees with Spinozism as well as
Leibniz' system does; and it is difficult to say which one
of the two founders may be playing the better joke on
us - and himself; although they mean it well!...
Mendelssohn has clearly demonstrated [= in the third of
his *Philosophische Gespräche*] that the *harmonia
praestabilita* is to be found in Spinoza. From this alone
it would follow that even more of Leibniz' fundamental
doctrines must be found in Spinoza, otherwise, Leibniz
and Spinoza (who could scarcely have been touched by
Wolff's lecturing) would not have been the kindred
spirits they unquestionably were. I dare say that I can
derive from Spinoza the whole of Leibniz' doctrine of
the soul .... Basically, both professed the same doctrine
of freedom and it is only an optical illusion that makes
their theories appear different. Whereas Spinoza (*Epist.*
LXII, *Opp. Posth.*, pp. 584 and 585) illustrates our sense
of freedom with the example of a thinking stone that is
conscious of doing its utmost to continue its movement,
Leibniz for his part does the same (*Theod.* § 50) by using
the example of a magnetic needle that would like to
point North believing that it could move independent of
any other first cause because it was unaware of the
imperceptible movement of magnetic matter.

   ... Leibniz explains finality by an *appetitus* [=
desire] or immanent *conatus* (conscientia sui praeditus) [=
a striving equipped with self-consciousness]. Spinoza did
likewise and understood it entirely in the same sense; for
him, the *representation of the external world* together
with *desire*, as for Leibniz, constitute *the essence of the
soul*.

---

[1] The first edition adds: "Moreover, I even feel as though somebody had picked my pocket."

In short, going to the heart of the matter, one finds in both Leibniz and Spinoza that every final cause always presupposes an efficient cause.... Thinking is not the source of substance - substance is the source of thinking. Therefore, Thinking must first be preceeded by a Not-thinking; a Not-thinking which must be posited as primordial if not entirely in reality, at least in its representation, its essence, its inner nature. In all honesty then, Leibniz could call souls "des automates spirituels." But how on earth could the principle of all souls *exist* by itself and *act* (I am arguing here in Leibniz' sense, at its most profound and most comprehensive level, as far as I understand it); how could spirit exist before matter, the idea before the object - that Gordian knot, which he should have untied in order to help us out of our predicament, he leaves just as tangled as it was....

Lessing: I won't let you rest until you make this parallelism public [= between Spinoza and Leibniz].... Aren't people always saying nowadays that Spinoza is dead as a dodo...?

I: They would talk that way no matter what. To grasp Spinoza requires too long and persistent an effort of the mind. Anyone for whom a single line of the *Ethics* remains obscure has not really grasped him; no one has grasped him who fails to understand how deeply and firmly a man of such stature could believe in his own philosophy, a conviction he so often and forcefully demonstrated. Even at the end of his days he could write: "... non praesumo, me optimam *invenisse* philosophiam, *sed veram me intelligere scio*" [= I do not pretend to have discovered the best philosophy, but I know that I recognize the true one. Letter LXXVI to Albert Burgh[*]]. Few will have enjoyed such peace of mind or so celestial an understanding, as he reached through the crystal clarity of his mind.

---

[*] Spinoza saw a clear distinction between being-certain and not-doubting.

Lessing: And you are not a Spinozist, Jacobi!

I: No, on my honour!

Lessing: If you follow your philosophy, you ought indeed, on your honour, to turn your back on all philosophy.

I: Why turn my back on all philosophy?

Lessing: If you don't, you are a total sceptic.

I: On the contrary, I draw back from a philosophy that makes a total scepticism necessary.

Lessing: But where do you go from there?

I: I follow the light which, Spinoza says, illumines both itself and the darkness. I love Spinoza because he, more that any other philosopher, has led me to believe firmly that certain things cannot be explained; things that we therefore cannot disregard but must take as we find them. I cling to no concept more passionately than to the concept of finality; I cling to no conviction with more fervour than to this: *I do what I think*, instead of *only thinking what I do*. In doing this, I must of course posit a source of thinking and action which remains for me totally inexplicable. But if I want to find an explanation for no matter what, I will come up against the second of the above propositions which, if it be carried to its ultimate consequences and applied to individual cases, is more than the human mind can bear.

Lessing: You express yourself almost as forthrightly as the decree of the Imperial Diet of Augsburg [= decree of the catholic majority at the Diet of 1530], but I am still an honest Lutheran and will stand by the "the more brutish than human error and the blasphemy that there is no free will," a statement with which the pristine mental clarity of your Spinoza would have felt comfortable.

I: But when talking about human behaviour, Spinoza had to
          twist and turn mightily in order to conceal his fatalism,
          especially in the fourth and fifth sections [= of *Ethics*],
          where I think he at times stoops to sophistry. And that
          precisely was my argument: even the best of minds will
          concoct   absurdities   when   it   attempts   to   explain
          everything, no matter what - to reconcile things by
          means of clear conceptualizations, to the total disregard
          of all else.

Lessing: And what about someone to whom explaining does not
          matter?

I: Anyone who does not attempt to explain the inexplicable,
          but simply to know the line of demarcation where the
          inexplicable begins, simply to recognize its presence: such
          a person, I think, has created within himself the
          maximum space for the harbouring of human truth.

Lessing: Words, words, my dear Jacobi! The line you wish to draw
          cannot be drawn. And besides, you are giving free rein
          to nonsense, fancies, blindness.

I: I think, it is possible to find such a line of demarcation.
          To *draw* it is not my intent, simply to discover the one
          already there and let it be. As far as nonsense, fancies,
          blindness are concerned....

Lessing: They find their dwelling wherever confused concepts
          prevail.

I: They are even more at home wherever *deceitful* concepts
          prevail. There we find enthroned the blindest, the most
          foolish, not to say the most stupid of beliefs. For if
          anyone ever becomes infatuated with a certain type of
          explanation, he will accept blindly all conclusions
          following from it; he is powerless to resist the
          compulsion for consistency, even if that consistency
          means he must needs stand on his head.

          ... In my own judgment a scholar's greatest merit is
          to unveil, to reveal *existence*.... To explain is for him

simply a means, a pathway to an end - the proximate, but never the ultimate goal. His ultimate goal is that which cannot be explained: whatever is insoluble, whatever is immediate, whatever is simple.

... Uncontrolled addiction to explaining would make us seek generalizations with such passion that in doing so, we ignore the particularities; it is our constant desire to integrate, where to separate might prove infinitely more profitable.... It happens too that in *pulling* things *together* and *connecting* only what can be explained about them, a certain flash of light appears in the soul that dazzles more than enlightens it. When that happens, we are sacrificing to a lower order of knowledge what Spinoza calls, profoundly and sublimely, the highest class of knowledge; for our eyes to observe more precisely, we shut the eyes of the soul, with which it contemplates God and itself....

Lessing: Good, very good! That's all very helpful to me; but it does not help me in the same fashion. All in all, I find your *salto mortale* not bad and I can see how a man with a head on his shoulders might have to turn a somersault in order to get moving ahead. Take me with you if that is possible.

I: If you will just jump onto this springboard from which I am launched [= see above the motto *dos moi pou sto*], that's all you need to do.

Lessing: Even to do that would entail a leap I may no longer ask of my old legs and my muddled head.

The conversation, reproduced here in outline, was followed by others which kept leading us back to the same topics by various routes.

Lessing once said with the trace of a smile that perhaps he himself was the Highest Being, present in the state of extreme contraction. I pleaded for my life. He answered that I had nothing to worry about and explained his thoughts in a way that reminded me of Henry Moore and F. Mercurius van Helmont (*philosophus per unum in quo omnia*) [= two 17th century theosophists]. He became even more explicit, to the point that, if pressed, I could well accuse him yet again of indulging in Cabbala. That gave him no small pleasure; that is why I seized the opportunity to speak for the kibbel, or Cabbala, in the *strictest sense and from the following point of view*: that in and of itself it is impossible to construct [erfinden] the infinite on the basis of a given finite, and then to grasp and somehow to formulate their mutual inter-relationship. It follows that any statement on that topic has to ensue from revelation. Lessing was adamant, "insisting that everything be seen in terms of the natural" [daß er sich alles "natürlich ausgebeten haben wollte"]; I, for my part, asserted that there can be no natural philosophy of the supranatural and yet the two (the natural and the supranatural) are obviously givens.

When Lessing wanted to imagine a *personal* divinity, he thought of it as the soul of the universe, and he thought of the Whole as being analogous to an organic body. The universal soul, therefore, *qua soul*, would be nothing but effect, as are all other souls in any conceivable system.[*] But the organic extension of the soul could not be thought of as analogous to the organic *parts* of that extension inasmuch as there could be nothing outside it to which it could refer, nothing from which it could take anything and nothing to which it could give anything back. Therefore, in order to continue to exist at all, it would have to retire, so to speak, into itself from time to time; it would have to unite within itself life, death, and resurrection. But of course one might variously imagine the inner economy of such a being.

Lessing was fascinated by that idea and applied it to all kinds of cases both seriously and in jest. Once, when we were dining at Gleim's home in Halberstadt (Lessing had accompanied me there after my second visit to him), it suddenly started raining and Gleim expressed his regrets because we had intended to retire to the garden after the meal; Lessing, who was sitting beside me, said:

---

[*] According to Leibniz' system as well. The entelechy becomes *spirit* only through the *body* (or the concept of the body).

"You know, Jacobi, maybe it is *I* who am doing this"[*] [= raining]. I answered: "Or perhaps it is *I*." Gleim raised his eyebrows at this but did not ask what we meant.[1]

Lessing could not abide the idea of a personal, truly infinite being perpetually enjoying its most supreme perfection. He associated with it an image of such *infinite boredom* that the very thought of it caused him pain and dread.

He believed that a continuation of man's personal life after death was not unlikely. He told me he had encountered certain ideas in Bonnet [= Swiss philosopher (1720-1793)], whom he was just reading, ideas which concurred with his on this matter and indeed with his system in general. Given the course of the conversation and my detailed knowledge of Bonnet (whose complete works I then knew almost by heart), I refrained from pursuing the matter; and since, for me, Lessing's system was anything but obscure or uncertain, I never thought of looking up Bonnet for confirmation until latterly when the matter at hand led me to do so. The work of Bonnet which Lessing had been reading at the time was surely none other than the *Palingénésie* [= *Palingénésie philosophique, ou Idées sur l'état passé et sur l'état futur des êtres vivants* (1769)], which you know very well; Paragraph VII of the 1st Part together with Section XIII of Paragraph IV of the *Contemplation de la nature* [= 1764], to which Bonnet there refers, probably contains the ideas Lessing had in mind. I am struck by a passage (p. 246 of the first edition, in French) where Bonnet says: "Seroit-ce qu'on imagineroit que l'univers seroit moins *harmonique*, j'ai presque dit, moins *organique*, qu'un *Animal?*"

---

[*] In the sense that one says: I am digesting, I am secreting good or harmful digestive juices, and so forth.

[1] Instead of the last sentence, the first edition has: "Gleim looked at us as though we were being silly; during the 3 x 24 hours we spent at his home he had the devil's own time with us yet never tired of countering us with his serene, ingenious, and brilliant humour, his jocularity and pleasant wit which was, though pointed, always kind."

On the day I took leave of Lessing to continue my journey to Hamburg, we were again conversing long and hard about all these matters. We were not far apart in our philosophy, differing only in point of faith. I gave Lessing three works by the philosopher Hemsterhuis: *Lettre sur l'homme et ses rapports* [= 1772], *Sophile* [= *Sophile, ou de la Philosophie* (1778)], and *Aristée* [= *Aristée, ou de la Divinité* (1779)]; he knew nothing by him save the *Letter on Sculpture* [= 1769]. It was with some reluctance that I gave him the *Aristée*, which I had just obtained when passing through Münster, but not yet read; Lessing's eagerness was too great.*

On my return I found Lessing so totally taken by that same *Aristée* that he was determined to translate it himself. It was pure Spinozism, Lessing said, clothed in such a beautiful, exoteric wrap that the wrap itself aided the explication and elucidation of the teaching contained within. I protested that, from what I knew of Hemsterhuis (I didn't know him personally at the time), he was no Spinozist; Diderot himself had assured me of this. "Read the book," replied Lessing, "and you will doubt no longer. His *Lettre sur l'homme et ses rapports* was still a bit hesitant and it's possible that Hemsterhuis himself didn't fully recognize his own Spinozism at that time; but he is most certainly aware of it now."

---

* Lessing had accompanied me to Braunschweig and it so happened that we parted that evening without saying farewell. Lessing wrote me a note which I did not receive but which he then handed to me on my return. Since it is not totally irrelevant to the thread of my narrative and appears to be of some documentary value, it may find its proper place here even if it is without any further significance.

Dear Jacobi,

I was not *meant* to bid you farewell in person. I do not *want* to do it in writing. Or what amounts to the same thing and spares me the puerile antithesis: I *am* not to.

My thoughts will be with you more often than not. How, after all, can people be together except in thought?

Have a safe journey and come back healthy and merry. Meanwhile, I want to do everything I can to make it possible to accompany you then.

My best regards to your sister.

Yours,

Lessing

Wolfenbüttel, July 11th, 1780.

You would have to be as conversant with Spinoza as was Lessing not to find this judgment paradoxical. What he called the exoteric wrap of the *Aristée* can correctly be viewed as a simple development of the doctrine of the indivisible, internal, and eternal conjoining of the infinite with the finite; of the universal, (as yet) indeterminate power with the determinate particular power; and of the necessary contrariety in their directions. The rest of the *Aristée* could well be used by a Spinozist. However, let me attest here most solemnly that Hemsterhuis is certainly no Spinozist; on the contrary, he is totally opposed to the essentials of that doctrine.

At that point Lessing had not yet read Hemsterhuis' essay *Sur les désirs*. It had arrived in a packet at my address just as I happened to be away.* Lessing wrote me he had been so plagued by impatience and curiosity that he had finally broken open the wrapping, and the rest of the contents he sent on to me at Kassel. "Of the work itself which gives me uncommon pleasure," he added, "I will write you later."

On December 4th, not long before his death, he did write to say: "In reading *Woldemar* [= Jacobi's novel written in 1779] I am reminded that I had undertaken to tell you my thoughts on Hemsterhuis' theory of love. You cannot believe how closely his thoughts relate to a theory which, in my opinion, actually explains nothing and which, to speak with the analysts [= the mathematicians], seems to me simply a substitution of one formula for another, which is more apt to lead me astray than to bring me closer to a solution. - But am I now in any position to write what I want to? - I am not even in a position to write what I have to, etc."** Before I became acquainted with Lessing's opinions, as

---

* During my first stay in Wolfenbüttel I had had to write for it to satisfy Lessing's great desire to see the work.
** Here is the letter in its entirety, perhaps one of Lessing's last.

Wolfenbüttel, December 4, 1780

Dear Jacobi,
    Langer, who has just sent me a letter from Amsterdam, may have told you that

reported above, and firmly convinced by documentary evidence that Lessing was an orthodox theist,[1] some passages of his *Education of the Human Race* had been quite inexplicable to me, especially §73. I

---

when he left me I intended to travel to Hamburg. I stayed there as long as I still thought I could hope among old friends to restore my lost health and good cheer. I have even forgotten how long that lasted. To be sure, I should have given it up sooner, this hope of mine. But who likes to do that unless he is forced to? A short time ago, I finally returned. Physically, I must say I am a little better, except for my eyes; but mentally much more unfit. Unfit for anything requiring the slightest effort.

Would I not otherwise have written you long since? May you read my soul as skillfully as I make bold to read yours. I know full well that it must upset you to set down yet again what you have already written to ***... (the omitted passage concerns my political situation at the time). There is nothing of yours I would read with more pleasure than your own *apologia*. To my mind, a man of your stamp is never in the wrong, however much he appear so in the eyes of the whole world - *with which he should not*, I repeat: not, *have become entangled* in the first place. My dear Jacobi, turn your mind from political preoccupations; go and sit down at your desk, and bring your *Woldemar* to its conclusion.

In reading *Woldemar* I am reminded that I had undertaken to tell you my thoughts on Hemsterhuis' theory of love. You cannot believe how closely his thoughts relate to a theory which, in my opinion, actually explains nothing and which, to speak with the analysts, seems to me simply a substitution of one formula for another, which is more apt to lead me astray than to bring me closer to a solution. - But am I now in any position to write what I want to? - I am not even in a position to write what I have to.

Nevertheless, there is *one* thing I still have to do; I still have to find out: did D. [= the devil] himself take complete possession of the clergy in Jülich and Berg? I think you are probably the one who sent me the *Proclama* [= *Proclama der Jülich-und Bergischen Evangelisch-Lutherischen Kirchen-Synode*, which threatened to punish anyone absenting himself from the church; after Daunicht, *Lessing*, p. 553], or whatever the abomination is called. My God! what contemptible people! They deserve to be suppressed once again by the Papacy and be subjected to the cruelest of Inquisitions. Do let me hear any more you may know of this most un-Lutheran manoeuvre.

Remember me to all your family, especially to the ones I know. That we are differently disposed to people we have met and those we have not met, "is not something *I* made up", you probably know this already (these last words refer to a passage in Hemsterhuis' *Sur les désirs*).

Tell your esteemed brother, who will soon be travelling through here again, that D. is not at home and all inns except mine are closed because of the plague.

[1] The first edition has: "deist."

would like to know how anyone can make sense of this passage without recourse to Spinozist ideas. With these, however, the commentary becomes straightforward. Spinoza's God is the pure principle of reality in all that is real, the principle of *being* in all that exists, entirely without individuality, simply and plainly infinite. The unity of that God rests upon the unity of that which cannot be differentiated and hence does not exclude a kind of plurality. But taken *merely* in this transcendental unity, the divinity must, as a matter of course, lack reality, which can be found expressly nowhere but in definite individual entities. Therefore, *reality*, along with our concept of it, rests upon the *natura naturata* (the Son from all eternity), while *possibility* (*the essence, the substantial of the infinite*), along with our concept of it, rests upon the *natura naturans* (the Father). *

What I earlier was at some pains to present concerning the spirit of Spinozism, would, I think, make any further exposition here superfluous.

You know as well as I do that these more or less confused representations have, since remotest antiquity, assumed manifold metaphoric shapes in coming to dwell amongst humankind. - "Here, to be sure, language lags behind concepts" [*Education*, §73, conclusion] just as one concept may lag behind another.

Many can bear witness that Lessing frequently and emphatically referred to the *Hen kai Pan* as being the quintessence of his theology and philosophy. He used the words as his favorite motto, on occasion putting them in writing. That is the formulation written down on the wall of Gleim's summerhouse beneath a motto of my own.[1]

---

* I request the reader not to spend much time on this commentary, which is too condensed and hence extremely obscure. The matter will become clear enough in the following letters.

[1] The first edition adds: "written in Lessing's own hand."

  The first and second editions both have: "Much relevant information might well be learned from Marquis Lucchesini. He was in Wolfenbüttel shortly before me, and Lessing praised him full-somely as being very clear-headed."

What I have recounted is not a tenth of what I could have related, had my memory assisted me sufficiently in point of wording and expression. It is for that reason that I kept Lessing's actual words to the bare minimum, in what I did report. When people converse for days on many and very varied topics, they are bound to forget detail. In addition, since I knew beyond the shadow of a doubt that "Lessing does not believe in a cause of things, which is distinct from the world"; or that "Lessing is a Spinozist", whatever he later said on the topic and however differently he put it impressed me no more than anything else did. To attempt to memorize his exact words never crossed my mind; it appeared to me quite conceivable that Lessing was a Spinozist. Had he affirmed the opposite, an affirmation which my intellectual curiosity was half expecting, I would most probably be able still to account for every significant word.

This, my most excellent sir, should satisfy a good part of what you required from me. But there are still one or two questions of yours I should like to touch upon briefly.

The questions, my most excellent sir, I must confess, took me rather aback because they presuppose on my part a state of ignorance - not to use a stronger word - in which I *could* perhaps find myself, but there was no external evidence there that could arouse in you the merest suspicion of such ignorance, let alone allow you to express that suspicion with such nonchalance.

You ask, "Did Lessing come right out and say: I believe Spinoza's system to be true and well founded?" And "Which system?" you ask. "Is it the one propounded in his *Tractatus theologico-politicus*, or the one in his *De principiis philosophiae cartesianae*, or the one Ludovicus Mayer circulated under Spinoza's name after his death?"

Anyone who knows even the slightest thing about Spinoza knows the story of his demonstration of Descartes' doctrine and knows moreover that it has nothing to do with Spinozism.

I know nothing of a system of Spinoza which you claim Ludovicus Mayer made known after Spinoza's death; unless you are thinking of the *Opera posthuma* themselves. Or perhaps only of the Preface; and Lessing, you would claim, made mock of me by foisting upon me the interpretation of Spinozism found there as his credo? But that really would be too much! Suppose it is the *Opera posthuma*, then I cannot see, if this is the case, how you can in any way *oppose* the *Tractatus theologico-politicus* to them. Spinoza's posthumous works are in complete agreement with what the *Tractatus* contains of his system. Till the end of his days he repeatedly referred to the *Tractatus*, explicitly and in a variety of contexts.

"Did Lessing," you go on to ask, "understand the system with the mis-understanding of a Bayle or with the better understanding of some others?"

There is a difference between understanding and *not-misunderstanding*. Bayle did not misunderstand Spinoza's system as far as its conclusions are concerned; one can only say that he did not understand *sufficiently whence they come*, that he did not *appreciate* their premises as the author had. If Bayle did misunderstand Spinoza (the reproach you make him), then, by the same token, Leibniz misunderstood him even *more*. Be so good as to compare Bayle's exposition *in the first lines* of note N [= of the article "Spinoza" in his *Dictionnaire historique et critique*] with what Leibniz said of Spinoza's doctrines in §§31, Praefatio Theod. 173, 374, 393. But if a Leibniz and a Bayle did not misunderstand Spinoza's system, there were others who certainly misunderstood it even though they thought they explained it better; or else, they twisted it. The latter are surely not in my camp and I vow that they were surely not in Lessing's either.

Lessing never lectured me formally with the words: "Dear brother mine, that much maligned Spinoza may well etc."

My dearest and most esteemed Mendelssohn, you should not take amiss the fact that my criticisms are so direct and unadorned, yes, perhaps even a bit caustic. When dealing with a man I respect so highly, this seemed the only proper tone.

I remain etc.

......

I received from Elise R. the following report concerning my letter's reception.

December 5, 1783

"Two post-days have passed, my dear Jacobi, since I received a provisional answer from our friend Mendelssohn. I could not inform you of it immediately because of a minor indisposition; and I could not send you the letter itself because my brother would not part with it since much of the letter was intended for him. *

"First, Mendelssohn frankly admits that he *misjudged you* because he 'discovers, not an amateur at philosophy, but a man who has made thinking his chief business and who possesses the strength to throw off the reins and go his own way.' There is so much philosophical acumen evident in the structure you have built on your own that he can well understand why Lessing was so enthusiastic and why he was able to place such unbounded confidence in its architect. For the present, you have answered his questions satisfactorily; you are justified in being annoyed with him, and he is prepared to ask your pardon.

Meanwhile, since your essay calls for a careful review at greater leisure, he asks me to make his excuses for taking more time to respond. But, before he writes about Lessing's character he will ask for further explication of various points in your essay. For the moment it is utterly impossible for him to give thought to either Lessing or Spinoza. He would prefer to do it later rather than badly; ultimately, however, it will be really up to you and all of us together to decide what use is to be made of this conversation with Lessing.

"*He for his part*, Mendelssohn continues, still agrees that in all fairness it is necessary and proper to warn those who love to speculate, and to indicate to them by means of *forceful* instances

---

* Before sending my letter to Mendelssohn, Elise showed it to her brother, J.A.H. Reimarus. He was of the opinion that Lessing's Spinozism ought not to become public knowledge and had written to Mendelssohn to that effect. His letter was enclosed with mine.

the danger to which they expose themselves when they indulge in their speculation without any guidance.

Whether *outsiders*, as a result, *are gladdened or saddened by what they will read* is no concern of ours;[1] it is not our intent to factionalize the issue, nor to recruit, nor to induce anyone to take sides; for, by soliciting and trying to create a faction, we would be veritable traitors to the cause to which we are sworn.

"There you have it, my dear Jacobi, this is the complete section from Mendelssohn's letter which touches upon Lessing and Spinoza."

———

Seven months then passed without a single word from Mendelssohn. Since during all that time fate was dealing me a series of harsh blows, I could give little thought to the matter; my correspondence, never an avid pursuit of mine, came to a standstill. Meanwhile it so happened that a statement about Spinoza from my friend Hemsterhuis prompted me to sketch a debate between the latter and Aristée. I drafted a conversation in June 1784, but from week to week delayed enclosing it in a letter and sending it off to Hemsterhuis.

Just about then a letter from Elise arrived with the news that Mendelssohn had decided to put aside for the moment his plan to write on Lessing's character in order this Summer to risk a bout with the Spinozists, or *Whole-Oners* [All Einer] as he chose to call them, health and time permitting. My friend Elise congratulated me for having occasioned with my essay such a useful work, since it is certainly most imperative to dispel the glaring errors of our

---

[1] Elise adds in the margin: "This refers to my brother's letter" [= letter of Nov. 11, 1783 to Mendelssohn in M. Mendelssohn, *Gesammelte Schriften* Vol. 13, pp. 155-156, where we read: "Our friend Lessing's judgment was indeed not always the most sound, the most precise, and the most clear since his vivid imagination deceived him at times in different ways; his passions together with a certain ill-humour caused him to fall prey to wild imaginings. You will know best how to present the matter - I would think, not in too much detail, so as to give no cause for rejoicing to those who stand outside and do not appreciate the human heart with all due humanity."]

times by the dazzling light of *pure reason* held on high in so steady a hand.

Most pleased with Mendelssohn's decision, I answered by return mail, whereupon I managed my letter to Hemsterhuis, thus clearing and freeing my mind of the whole affair.

At the end of August I travelled to Hofgeismar to restore my debilitated health and to revive my spirits in the company of two of the best and kindest persons, Princess von Gallitzin and Freiherr von Fürstenberg. While there, I received an unexpected letter from Mendelssohn, which included comments on the philosophy expounded in my essay. The packet had arrive unsealed at the home of our mutual friend Elise, who then placed it in an envelope; it had reached Düsseldorf just after my departure.

Berlin, August 1, 1784

To Herr Jacobi, in Düsseldorf,

Elise has already let you know on my behalf that I was very much put to shame by your philosophical letter and, in the foreword this deserving friend enclosed for my benefit, you were so kind as to forgive me the precipitous manner with which I attacked your initial communication. One is so used to encountering philosophical masks and mummers that, in the end, like Shaftesbury's Ethiopian [= see below p. 127], one runs the risk of thinking every honest face a mask.

I have since read your essay repeatedly, to familiarize myself with your own peculiar train of thought. After the fiftieth year of our life, the mind is not at all amenable to being led along a new path. Even though it may follow a guide for some distance, it will welcome any opportunity to return to its usual track, thereby imperceptibly losing sight of its guide. This may be the reason why one or the other passage in your letter is utterly incomprehensible and why I fail at some points to see how your thoughts are consonant with your argument.

Since for the moment I have completely set aside my project to write of Lessing and wish first to draft something on Spinozism, you will see how important it must perforce be for me to grasp your ideas correctly and to understand duly the reasons for which you are at such pains to lend support to the system of that philosopher. I therefore take the liberty of submitting my critiques and comments in the enclosed essay. You have thrown down the gauntlet; I accept your challenge; let us now begin a metaphysical tournament and battle it out, as did knights of old, before the eyes of the lady we both so highly esteem. It will be an enviable thing to receive the victor's prize from her hands, but it would not prove altogether grievous to win her sympathy if one loses. Elise will send this missive on to you and beg the favour of a reply.

Moses Mendelssohn

Comments for the Attention of Herr Jacobi[1]

"Something is posited out of nothing," you say, "by anything that originates within the infinite, in whatever metaphors one might cloak it, or by each and every change within the infinite"; you believe that Spinoza "rejected any *transition* from the infinite to the finite; he rejected transient causes altogether, be they secondary or remote. In the place of the emanating One he posited an Ensoph that was *immanent* only: an inherent cause of the world, eternally unchangeable *in itself*, which, taken together with all that followed from it, would be One and the Same." Here I come up against certain difficulties I cannot myself resolve.   1) If a series without beginning seemed not impossible to Spinoza, then even the emergence of things by way of emanation does not necessarily lead to a *becoming out of nothing*.   2) If for Spinoza those things are something finite, then their inherence in the infinite can be understood no more easily, in fact, I think less easily, than can their emanation from it. If the infinite cannot cause anything finite, then neither can it think [denken] anything finite.

On the whole Spinoza's system does not seem to lend itself to resolving these kinds of difficulty. They must arise though, in respect both of the ideas and of their real objects. What cannot become objectively real, cannot be subjectively thought. Spinoza

---

[1] Included by Jacobi in the second and the last editions, they are here taken from Mendelssohn's *An die Freunde Lessings* (1786).

encounters the same difficulty in letting the finite really exist outside God; I say, he will again come upon the same difficulty when he transposes the finite into the divine essence and sees it as a thought of the divinity.

Subsequently, you explain a passage in Spinoza which Lessing called his most obscure and which Leibniz found equally so, failing indeed to understand it completely; viz.: "The infinite cause as such, as you express it, is explicitly devoid of both reason and will; for, as a consequence of its transcendental unity and constant absolute infinity, it cannot have any object of thinking and willing." Furthermore, you declare that you intend only to deny particular ideas and particular determinations of the will to that first cause, which is infinite in nature; and you give as your reason, that every particular concept must spring from another particular concept and be directly related to an actually existing object. Thus, you want to allow to the first cause only the initial, internal, general prime matter [Urstoff] of reason and of will.

I must confess that I understand this explanation as little as I do the words of Spinoza himself. The first cause has ideas [Gedanken] but no understanding [Verstand]. It has ideas - for ideas are, according to Spinoza, one of the main attributes of the unique true substance. Yet it possesses no particular ideas, only their general prime matter. What generality can be grasped in isolation from particularity? Surely this is even more incomprehensible than formless matter, prime matter without form [Urstoff ohne Bildung], a being that has only general characteristics but no particular one? Absolute infinity, you assert, has no object of thought. But is it not in itself, are not its attributes and modifications themselves, objects of thought? If it has no object of thought, no understanding, how can thought be at the same time its attribute? how can it be at the same time the only thinking substance? Furthermore, where its modifications, or accidental things, really possess particular determinations of the will, would the substance itself possess merely the general prime matter of the will? In Spinoza at least I half understand this. He views free will as merely consisting of an indeterminate choosing, devoid of intent, of that which is perfectly indifferent. To the extent that the divinity is represented as a finite being, it seemed possible to him to attribute this choice to the modification of the divinity; but to the extent that it is an infinite being, Spinoza justly denies the divinity itself such an intentional freedom. According to him, the knowledge of the good by which a free choice is effected belongs integrally to the attributes of understanding; and to that extent it is of the most certain necessity; hence the consequences - whether they proceed from the knowledge of the true and the false, or from the knowledge of good and evil - must all be equally necessary. Yet since you, sir, accept the system of the determinists and allow humankind itself no other choice but the choice which springs from the last practical consideration of all motives and driving forces, then I do not see why you deny to the infinite cause such a choice, pre-determined from all eternity. To the extent that you deny true individuality to the infinite, it can be granted neither will nor freedom - quite true; for both of these presuppose real individual substantiality. However, this is not the reason you adduce and as a result this seems to me to be in total contradiction to Spinoza's system as I will soon have occasion to elaborate.

To follow Spinoza's concepts: everything that occurs in the visible world is of the strictest necessity because that is how it is grounded in the divine nature and in the possible modifications of its attributes. Whatever does not happen in actuality is for him not even possible, not thinkable. Therefore, had Spinoza conceded (as Bayle, Leibniz and others thought) that only the principle of contradiction provides inner possibility with a goal, then he would of necessity have taken for real all the occurrences in the novels of Scudéry and fictions of Ariosto, as Leibniz aptly reminds us concerning the passage quoted. But Spinoza also considered impossible anything which, though devoid of contradiction, was still not grounded in the modifications of the divine as the necessary cause of all things. You can see here the path by which Spinoza himself would have reached the *perfectissimum*, if he had been able to accommodate himself to the determinists' concept of freedom. Only according to this system of the *perfectissimum* is it conceivable why, within divine nature, no other series of determinations but this became real, or as Spinoza would have put it, why no other series was possible.

What you subsequently say about *sequence* and *duration* has my complete approval; except that I would not state that they are *mere illusion*. They are necessary determinations of our limited thinking: that is, *appearances*, which one must, to be sure, distinguish from mere illusion.

Your *salto mortale* constitutes one of nature's salutary pathways. After a long chasing through thorns and thickets in pursuit of speculation, I always try to orientate myself with the *bon sens* and take care to look for the pathway and see where I can rejoin it. Since I cannot deny that intentions exist, then to have intention is one possible attribute of the spirit; and to the degree that it is not a mere absence of capacity, it must belong eminently to every spirit; furthermore, alongside thinking, a willing and a doing exist which, since they can, must be attributes of the infinite.

The ingenious stroke, with which Lessing responds, is entirely in his style; one of his pranks in which he gave the appearance of vaulting out of his own skin, as it were, and did in actual fact not budge an inch. To wonder whether there is not something that not only surpasses all concepts but lies totally outside the concept: this I call vaulting out of one's own skin. My credo is: what I cannot conceive of as true does not, *qua* doubt, cause me unease. Nor can I answer a question I do not understand; it is for me tantamount to no question at all. It never entered my head to try to climb onto my own shoulders in order to obtain the broader view.

In one of his comedies, Lessing has a character, a believer in magic, say of a burning light: "This light isn't really burning, but only seems to burn; it isn't really shining, but only seems to shine" [es scheint nur zu scheinen]. The first negation has some basis; but the second refutes itself. What appears to be, must appear to be real. Every phenomenon, as a phenomenon is eminently evident. Viewed subjectively, all ideas are of consummate truth. So the power to think is a really elemental power which cannot be grounded in a higher original power. You yourself do not seem to have attached any special importance to this bizarre fancy of our friend Lessing.

When you say, however, "Spinoza's infinite unique substance, by itself and aside from the particular things, has no definite, complete existence," then you completely confound the whole idea of Spinozism I had worked out. So according to that system, particular things have a real, definite existence, and their *Together* is only *One* without having any definite, complete existence? How am I to understand this? Or to reconcile it with the rest of your statements?

If, as you mention later, Spinoza thought about freedom the same way Leibniz did, then he also would have had to agree that the knowledge of good and evil cannot, considering the most perfect first cause, be without consequences any more than can the knowledge of truth and error; he would have had to agree further that the most perfect first cause has to be pleased with good, displeased with evil - which is the same as saying that it would have to have intentions and, when it is acting, would have to act according to intentions.

Here once again is the point at which the scholastic philosopher greets the Spinozist with a fraternal embrace.

I come upon another passage of your essay, one totally incomprehensible to me, where you say, "Thinking is not the source of substance - substance is the source of thinking. Therefore, Thinking must first be preceded by a Not-thinking which must be posited as primordial if not entirely in reality, at least according to its representation, its essence, its inner nature." - Here you, along with our friend, seem to me to be trying to think something which is not a thought, to leap into a void whither reason [Vernunft] cannot follow. You want to think *something* that precedes all thinking and thus is unthinkable even to the most perfect intellect [Verstand].

The source of all those pseudo-concepts, it would seem to me, is that you consider extension and movement the sole matter and object of thought, and even these only to the extent that they actually do exist. I do not see why you presume this to be an established fact. Can the thinking being not be to itself matter and object? We know how we feel when we endure pain, hunger, thirst, frost, or heat; when we fear, hope, love, despise something, etc. However you call them: ideas, concepts, or perceptions and affections of the soul, it is enough that, with all these affections, the soul has neither extension nor movement as its object. Indeed, in the case of sense perceptions, what do sound, odour, colour, what does the sense of taste have to do with extension or movement? I know full well that *Locke* has accustomed philosophers to consider extension, impermeability, and movement to be *qualitates primitivae*, and to reduce to them the phenomena of the other senses as *qualitates secundariae*. But what reason has the Spinozist to accept this? In the end can there not also be a mind that conceives extension and movement simply as being possible, even though they do not exist in actuality? According to Spinoza, who considers extension to be an attribute of the unique infinite substance, this ought to be all the more acceptable.

I shall pass over a number of clever ideas with which our friend Lessing time and again entertained you and of which it is difficult to say whether they were intended as teasing or as philosophy. It was his whimsical habit to pair the most disparate ideas, just to see what kinds of offspring they would beget. To be sure, the random tossing about of ideas at times produced astounding observations of which he could afterwards make good use. But the majority of them were simply *quaint fancies*, which were always entertaining enough over a cup of coffee. Everything you have him say, toward the end of your report, deserves that label: his views on the economy of the world soul, on Leibniz' entelechies (supposedly a mere effect of the body), his fulminations, his *infinite boredom*, and similar thoughts which, like showers of fireworks, sparkle for a moment, crackle, and then vanish. I shall pass over too, without comment, the honourable retreat to the shelter of faith that you, for your part, propose. Such a proposal is entirely in keeping with the spirit of your religion which imposes an obligation to suppress doubt by means of faith. The Christian philosopher may amuse himself by teasing the natural philosopher [den Naturalisten] and by raising knotty puzzles that, like will-o'-the-wisps, lure him from one end of the field to the other, always eluding his surest grasp. My religion is under no obligation to remove such doubts in any way except by rational arguments; it commands no belief in eternal truths. And so I have even more reason to seek *conviction* [= by rational arguments].

I come next to the passage where you again try to clarify the principle of reality, following Spinoza. "Spinoza's God," you say, "is the pure principle of reality in all that is real, the principle of being in all that *exists*, entirely without individuality, simply and plainly *infinite*. The unity of that God rests upon the identity of that which cannot be differentiated and hence does not exclude a kind of plurality. But taken merely in this transcendental unity, the divinity must as a matter of course lack reality, which can be found expressly nowhere but in definite individual entities." - If I understand this correctly, only definite individual beings are really existing things; but the infinite, or principle of reality, consists only of the *Together*, of the *sum and substance* of all those individuals. Hence it is a mere *collectivum quid* [= collective whole] bereft of all substantiality except that of its constituent members. Now, every *collectivum* rests upon the idea that draws the manifold together; for except in thought (objectively), every individual being is isolated, *One* thing all by itself; relation-ship alone makes it into a part of the whole, a member of the *Together*. But relationship is an operation of thinking. Please help me overcome my confusion regarding Spinozism. I ask you firstly: wherein does that idea subsist, that *collectivum*, the relationship of the individual being to the whole? Not in the individual being; for each subsists only for its own part. If we deny this, we would have not only a kind of plurality in the divinity, but a true, numberless multiplicity. Again, it cannot subsist in a collective, for this would lead to obvious absurdities. Therefore, if that *Pan*, that Together, is to possess any truth at all, it must subsist in a real transcendental unity to the exclusion of all plurality; and this, against all expectation, lands us right back on the well-worn path of scholastic philosophy.

Furthermore: till now I had always thought that, according to Spinoza, the unique infinite alone had true substantiality, while the manifold finite was merely a modification, or idea, of the infinite. You seem to reverse all this. You grant the individual being true substantiality. If that be so, the whole would have to be simply the individual's idea. In so doing, you are chasing me around in a circle I cannot escape. For on other occasions you seem to agree with me that Spinoza allows only one transcendental infinite substance whose attributes are infinite extension and infinite ideas.

But the greatest difficulty I encounter in Spinoza's system lies for me in the fact that he will have it that the Unlimited results from the gathering in of all that which is limited.

How can degree be increased through addition? How can the intensive be increased through an *increase* of the extensive? Whereas in other systems the passage from infinite to finite is difficult to understand, in Spinoza's system the return of the finite into the intensive infinite seems to me utterly impossible. Intensity will never result from a simple increase, not even if the increase be infinite. If we attribute a quantity to the degree, then this is an intensive quantity which cannot be increased by the addition of like things. Would not a Spinozist here obviously have to change the concepts around, accepting as valid multiplicity instead of inner strength?

To some extent Wolff already touched upon this objection in Part II of his natural theology; though, to my knowledge, none of Spinoza's apologists has responded to it.

So much for Mendelssohn's *Comments*. Here is my answer.

Hofgeismar, September 5, 1784

To Herr Moses Mendelssohn, in Berlin

My ill health, which has been worsening for several months, has driven me to take the waters here and will in all probability send me even further on. The sulphurous fumes of the mineral waters, assailing me without and within, have rendered me quite unable to reply at once to your esteemed letter of August 1st (it did not arrive in Düsseldorf until the 27th and reached me here on September 1st). But a happy coincidence nevertheless places me in a position to give you forthwith certain satisfaction. Princess von Gallitzin, who is also taking the waters here, has brought a copy of the letter I sent to Hemsterhuis some time ago concerning Spinoza's philosophy. I am having a second copy made and am enclosing it. What I have to say in reply to the most important points of your *Comments* will be found here in a context which will shed more light upon the whole issue and dispel much misunderstanding. I actually recoiled in horror at your reproach that I consider extension and movement to be the only matter and object of thought. Nothing in the world could be further from my mind than such an opinion, and I fail to understand how I might have given you the slightest cause to ascribe to me such a thought.

As soon as I return home and am rested I shall re-read my report to you on Lessing, compare my statements with your *Comments*, and add belatedly things which still might not have been dealt with adequately in the essay I am enclosing. I know naught of any gauntlet that I am supposed to have thrown down. If I happen to have dropped a glove, and you insist on seeing it as a gauntlet and insist, furthermore, on taking this as a challenge - so be it; I will not ignore it but will defend myself as best I can. But what I stood for then and still stand for now is not Spinoza and his system, but Pascal's words: "La nature confond les pyrrhoniens et la raison confond les dogmatistes." I have made clear enough what and who I am; that you take me for someone else is not the result of any dissembling on my part. The combat and its outcome will make abundantly clear that I have made no use of knavish tricks and that the last thing that would occur to me would be to run and hide. I commend myself to heaven, to the gracious lady presiding over this tournament, and to the gentlemanly nature of my adversary.

> [Jacobi's letter to Hemsterhuis follows; it is the first of his three presentations of Spinoza's system.
> In Scholz, *Hauptschriften*, pp. 123-136]

...

I heard not a word from Mendelssohn the whole Winter. Then, in February, Elise sent me a copy of a letter she had just received from him and which, as she said, "was, to be sure, written to her, but *for* me." Herewith, the letter.

Berlin, January 28, 1785

Dearest Elise!

I do not in fact know any more whether I owe Herr Jacobi a reply or he me. A while ago, when he sent me through you a copy of his letter to Hemsterhuis, he promised me a further, specific response to my previous letter as soon as he left the spa and could find the requisite leisure. Has he since forgotten me? That I do not forget him but keep him in lively remembrance, I hope, God willing, to show him with a manuscript of some twenty-odd folios. You see, my dearest friend, you have brought me to this pass against my will. I haven't wanted to write at length for a long time now nor even write at all on metaphysical questions, and it is you I have to blame that I am now drowning in transcendental subtleties. I am working at a snail's pace; for my nervous debility doesn't permit any sustained effort, and domestic affairs consume most of my time and energy. Then too, these are so various in kind and fundamentally so foreign to my nature that they crush my spirit, shrivel my heart, and render me incapable of decent performance even when I am resting from them. And so, I cannot say how soon my manuscript will be in a state suitable for submission to Herr Jacobi. In the meantime I do what energies allow, and neither you nor Herr Jacobi would expect any more from an honest man.

Would he ever think of allowing someone to make public use of his philosophical letters? At present, my inquiry does not indeed relate to Spinozism alone but represents a kind of review of the usual proofs for the existence of God. Subsequently, however, I shall go into the basic premises of the Spinozist system more deeply; to do this, I would find it most convenient (and many of my readers very helpful) if I might make use of Herr Jacobi's vivid presentation and have him speak in Spinoza's stead. I would like to know soon, if at all possible, because I must organize my presentation accordingly.

In the meanwhile not one page of it is to be published without *our* [J.A.H.] Reimarus' having seen and approved it, etc.

———————

I wrote Mendelssohn post haste, granting him free use of my letters and promising him for the coming month without fail the specific response he was still awaiting.

Immediately afterwards, I was overcome by an illness from which I did not begin to recover 'til the end of March. I notified my friend Elise of the delay so that she might pass the news on to Mendelssohn and assure him at the same time that I was now hard at work.

I completed my essay on April 21th[1] and sent it by the next post with the following letter.

Düsseldorf, April 26, 1785

To Herr Moses Mendelssohn,

At my request Elise will have already notified you of the most recent difficulties which delayed my response to your *Comments*. I am now all the more seriously concerned to provide you satisfaction on the issue itself. In reference to my Introduction, I beg you not to think that I in all seriousness I might have taken anything from you in bad part.

I depart to-night to spend a few days in Münster and am on that account very busy and distracted, else I would be writing more as to the possible advantages there might be in presenting to the public Spinoza's system in its true form *and according to the intrinsic coherence of its parts*. Its spectre has been haunting Germany for lo these many years in all shapes and sizes and is regarded with reverence by believers and doubters alike. I am speaking not just of the petty-minded but of people with the finest minds....

Perhaps we will yet experience a controversy that will loom over Spinoza's bones like the one between the Archangel and Satan over Moses' remains.... There is more to follow on all this after I have your answer and know whether you can join with me on the interpretation of Spinoza's doctrine - I can hardly imagine that you would not.

Forgive this so hastily penned and disorganized letter; farewell, and may I rest assured of your good favour.

---

[1] The first edition has: "I completed my essay on April 21st. I omit the Introduction because it only contains the reasons why I deemed it good to contrast Mendelssohn's *Comments* simply with a new presentation of Spinoza's system, mainly *justifying my interpretation* of that system."

[At this point Jacobi's second presentation of Spinoza's doctrine follows; it is a series of forty-four statements along with their respective justification.
In Scholz, *Hauptschriften*, pp. 141-165]

...

With this, my presentation is at an end. I believe that, through this and the letter to Hemsterhuis, I have responded sufficiently to all the essential points in your *Comments*. In conclusion, I wish to address myself to a few passages referring to me personally and which I may not pass over in silence as I did some others.

"I shall," you say, "pass over a number of clever ideas with which our friend Lessing, time and again, entertained you and of which it is difficult to say whether they were intended as teasing or as philosophy.... Everything you have him say, toward the end of your report, deserves that label: his views on the economy of the world soul, on *Leibniz' entelechies being supposedly a mere effect of the body*, his fulminations, his infinite boredom, and similar thoughts which, like showers of fireworks, sparkle for a moment, crackle, and then vanish."

What stands in the letter is to the effect that Lessing said of the world soul: *assuming it does exist*, it can be, *qua soul*, only an effect (as are all other souls in all possible systems). I added in a footnote of my own, not as a quotation from Lessing: "According to Leibniz' system as well. The entelechy becomes *spirit* only through the body (or the concept of the body)." Which is of course something quite different from: "Leibniz' entelechies are a mere effect of the body."

In my first draft I had added to the footnote the following words from Leibniz.

[Here Jacobi quotes from *Principes de la nature et de la grâce fondés en raison*, Nos. 2 and 4, among others.]

...

Afterwards, I deleted the entire quotation as being superfluous, since it struck me that my assertion was so obviously grounded in Leibniz at every turn that, in spite of the incisive form I had given my assertion, one could not fail to recognize this fact, at least after some reflection.

"Likewise," you continue, " I shall pass over too, without comment, the honourable retreat to the shelter of faith that you, for your part, propose. Such a proposal is entirely in keeping with the spirit of your religion which imposes an obligation to suppress doubt by means of faith. The Christian philosopher may amuse himself by teasing the natural philosopher and by raising knotty puzzles that, like will-o'-the-wisps, lure him from one end of the field to the other, always eluding his surest grasp. My religion is under no obligation to remove such doubts in any way except by rational arguments; it commands no belief in eternal truths. And so I have even more reason to seek *conviction* [= by rational arguments]."

My dear Mendelssohn, we are all of us born within faith, and in faith we perforce continue, just as we are all born within society and in society we must needs continue. How can we strive toward certainty unless certainty is already known to us in advance? And how can it be known to us except through something we already recognize with certainty? This leads to the concept of an immediate certainty which not only needs no proof but even totally excludes all proofs, and which is purely and simply *the representation itself in conformity with the thing represented* (which in fact contains in itself its own reason). Conviction through proofs is a second-hand certainty and rests on comparison; it can never be altogether certain and total. Now, if every *taking-to-be-true* [Fürwahrhalten], which does not have its origins in rational grounds, is faith, then conviction based on rational grounds must itself come from faith and from faith alone must draw its strength.

It is through faith that we know we have a body and that other bodies and other thinking beings exist apart from us. A veritable and marvellous revelation! For, in fact, we perceive only our body, however it may be constituted; and by sensing it as being of a particular constitution, we become aware not only of its transformations but also of something totally distinct from it, which is neither pure perception nor idea; we become aware of *other real things*, and that, with the very same certainty with which we become aware of ourselves; for without a *Thou*, the I is impossible.

Thus we have a revelation of nature which does not merely demand but indeed compels each and everyone *to believe* and, through that faith, to accept eternal truths.

It is a different faith that is taught - and not demanded - by the religion of the Christians. A faith which deals not with eternal truths but with the finite contingent nature of the human being. It teaches him how he can acquire traits which will help him personally to progress to a higher life - ascending through it to a higher consciousness which leads in turn to higher knowledge. Whoever accepts that promise and advances steadfastly toward its fulfilment has the faith which ensures blessedness. That is why the sublime teacher of this faith, in whom all the promises of faith were already fulfilled, could say in truth: I myself am the way, the truth, and the life; no one comes to the Father save through me; but he who accepts the will which is in me will know that my teaching is true and is of God.

This, then, is the spirit of my religion: a human being becomes aware of God through a godly life; and there is a peace of God which passeth all understanding; in that peace dwells the bliss and vision of a love beyond all telling.

Love is life; *it is life itself*; it is only the type of love that differentiates between categories of living beings. He, *the Living God*, can manifest himself only in *that which is alive* and can make himself known to that which is alive only *through love which has been quickened*. This is the call of the voice crying in the wilderness: "In order to clear away humankind's never-ending *wrong relationship* with God, either they must become partakers of the divine; or God must assume flesh and blood." [J.G. Hamann]

Reason [Vernunft], which has become impoverished, speculative[1], *degenerate*, can neither accept nor tolerate that practical path. It

---

[1] The third edition has: "which has become *mere 'understanding'* [Verstand]."

has not the wherewithall to construct such a path and is too embarrassed to ask for help. That is why it must scurry around after truth which has run off together with intuitive understanding [schauender Verstand], and must limp behind religion and its trappings - just as morality does behind our vanished virtuous leanings, just as the law does behind the long-lost commonweal and higher morality, and just as pedagogics.... But let me interrupt this list for fear of being overwhelmed by the tidal wave rushing toward me.

May the spirit of truth be with us both.

Düsseldorf, April 21, 1785

Since I had already made Mendelssohn wait so long, I sent my packet this time directly to Berlin. On that same evening I set out on a journey; and so Elise, who already owed me a reply to two letters, was left without any news.

I received a letter from her on May 26th in which she related the following passage from Mendelssohn's response to the the news that I was bed-ridden for all of March: "I was just on the point of requesting you to ask our mutual friend not to be unduly hasty with his answer to my *Comments*. I have decided to have the first Part of my booklet printed after the Leipzig Book Fair. In it I deal to be sure *mainly with pantheism*; but still not a word is mentioned there concerning our correspondence. I am reserving this for the second Part, though it will not be ready for quite some time. Jacobi should read the first Part of my treatise before answering my *Comments*. Please extend greetings to my esteemed adversary."

It was but a month since I had sent Mendelssohn my most recent paper [= the second presentation of Spinoza's doctrine] and more than three months since I had promised him to send it without delay. As a result, the news that was meant to spare me my pains came rather a little late, albeit I had certainly not been overly expeditious.

I was still hoping for an answer from Mendelssohn. After waiting three months in vain, I found myself moved little by little to make my own decision and more and more inclined to bring to light, by means of the letters included here, such a presentation of Spinozism as seemed to me useful at the present juncture.

I therefore set about looking over my papers and excerpted from them the following brief statements in order, finally, to present them unambiguously as a summary of my claims.

[In the original, Jacobi's third presentation and critique of Spinozism follow in the form of six statements, together with their respective justification.
In Scholz, *Hauptschriften*, pp. 173-180.
Here only the statements are given.]

1. Spinozism is atheism.
2. Cabbalistic *philosophy* is, as *philosophy*, but an *undeveloped* Spinozism, or a version thereof, *confused anew*.
3. The Leibniz-Wolffian philosophy is no less fatalistic than the Spinozist philosophy and inevitably leads the persistent scholar back to its principles.
4. All ways of demonstration end in fatalism.
5. We can demonstrate only similarities (*agreements*, *conditionally necessary truths*, progressing in identical statements). Every proof presupposes something already proven, the first principle of which is *revelation*.
6. The prime element of all human knowledge and action is faith.

At the beginning of June, one of my friends [= Hamann] wrote me about the opus on which Mendelssohn was working and gave me as its title: *Morning Thoughts on God and Creation*, or *On the Existence and Attributes of God*.

That same friend went on to inform me that Mendelssohn's *Morning Thoughts* was in fact (he had been assured of it) already off the press already.[1]

---

[1] The first edition adds: "Upon reading this news I put my papers away until I might see my illustrious opponent's work; my own could obviously no longer appear at the same time as his. I made arrangements to obtain it as quickly as possible."

Soon afterwards I received from Mendelssohn the following letter, unsealed, within an envelope from our mutual friend Elise.

Berlin, July 21, 1785

Forgive me, my dearest Herr Jacobi, that I still have not responded to either of your important essays, the one in French to Hemsterhuis and the one in German to myself. Elise and her brother will attest that I have not been idle in our controversy, given the constraints of my present poor health; unless a Reimarus totally rejects my work, the upcoming Fair Catalogue will further confirm the testimony of those two witnesses. To be sure, I do not reckon that I shall with this work persuade you of my opinion; still less do I flatter myself that it is in my power to do so since, I must confess, so many passages in your essays as well as in the writings of Spinoza himself are utterly incomprehensible to me. But in the work very soon to be submitted for your evaluation I hope to establish the *status controversiae* and thereby give the debate its proper introduction. At least the reasons will become apparent why many points strike me as being absolutely incomprehensible; and why, the more you are at pains to explicate them for me, the more obscure they become.

And now, one further request. My papers are always in poor order and I have lost among them the copy of my *Comments* which I am certain I stored somewhere. I have already been searching in vain for some weeks; a search for lost papers is a task devoid of all pleasure. Perhaps you have it at hand and can let me have a copy at your convenience. I would be greatly obliged to you; for I am finally of a mind to get on with our controversy and, to that end, to read yet again both your essays with all the attention and energy I can muster. But for this, it is imperative that I have the *Comments* to which your response is addressed. Farewell, my dear fellow, and remain kindly affected towards me.

Moses Mendelssohn

A copy of the *Comments* was available and made it possible for me to answer Mendelssohn at once in fulfilment of his request.

There was no need to give any further thought to the course I had to follow. Since Mendelssohn had changed his mind about showing me his work in manuscript form and consigned it, all of a sudden, to the printer; since I had learnt even its title only by hearsay and was not to have it confirmed as a certainty until the *Fair Catalogue* appeared; and since Mendelssohn had *at this point* decided to establish a *status controversiae* in that very work - for all these reasons then, however great my boundless confidence in my adversary's honesty and best intentions had been and would remain, I could not possibly leave it up to him, unilaterally, "to give the debate its proper introduction and to show publicly the reasons why many points (in my essays) strike him as being absobutely incomprehensible and why, the more I am at pains to explicate them for him, the more obscure they become."

Still less could I permit a *status controversiae* to be established in which it would fall to me to play, so to speak, the *advocatus diaboli*, unless at the same time the whole occasion for the controversy was to be made public at the very outset. It was extremely important to me that it be perfectly clear in what sense I had taken Spinoza's part, that it had been purely and simply a case of one speculative philosophy against another speculative philosophy, or more correctly, of *pure metaphysics* against *pure metaphysics*. I use these words in their literal sense and not in the sense of the proverb: in fugam vacui [= I ran away (?)].

[Here follows Jacobi's critique of rationalism and Enlightenment, ending with a long quotation from Lavater.
In Scholz, *Hauptschriften*, pp. 183-201. -
And in the second and third editions, *Beylagen*.
In Scholz, *Hauptschriften*, pp. 203-282]

M. Mendelssohn, *An die Freunde Lessings. Ein Anhang zu Herrn Jacobis Briefwechsel über die Lehre des Spinoza*. Berlin 1786.

[From Scholz, *Hauptschriften*, pp. 291-325]

"If a native of Ethiopia were on a Sudden transported into Europe, and plac'd either at Paris or Venice at a time of Carnival, when the general face of mankind was disguis'd and almost every Creature wore a Mask; t'is probable he woul'd for some time be at a stand, before he discover'd the Cheat: not imagining that a whole People cou'd be so fantastical, as upon agreement, at an appointed time, to transform themselves by a Variety of Habits, and make it a Solemn Practice to impose on one another, by this universal Confusion of Characters and Persons. Tho he might at first perhaps have lookd on this with a serious eye, it wou'd be hardly possible for him to hold his Countenance, when he had percei'vd what was carrying on. The Europeans, on their Side, might laugh perhaps at this Simplicity. But our Ethiopian would certainly laugh with better reason. Tis easy to see which of the two wou'd be ridiculous, bear a double share of Ridicule. However, shou'd it so happen, that in the Transport of ridicule, our Ethiopian, having his Head still running upon Masks, and knowing nothing of the fair Complexion and Common Dress of the Europeans, should upon the Sight of a naturel face and Habit, laugh just as heartly as before: wou'd not he in his turn become ridiculous, by carrying the jest too far; when by a silly presumption he took Nature for mere Art, and mistook perhaps a Man of Sobriety and Sense for one of those ridiculous Mummers."

Shaftesbury, *Essay on the Freedom of Wit and Humour*. Part II, Sect. I.[1]

---

[1] Quoted in English by Mendelssohn; it is reproduced here exactly as found in Mendelssohn's text.
Instead of applying the image of the Ethiopian to himself, as he did above, Mendelssohn here applies it to Jacobi, who would mistake Lessing's mask for his face and Mendelssohn's face for a deceptive mask. (after Scholz)

Our friend's devotion to Spinozism is not to be seen as a mere hypothesis (as the Patriarch in *Nathan* puts it), postulated simply in order to discuss its pros and cons. Herr Jacobi, a man of established reputation in the Republic of Scholars, takes a public stand and asserts as fact: *Lessing was in effect and in actuality a Spinozist.* Proofs of this are supposedly to be found in correspondence between him, a third person, and myself, which, laid before the public in a court of inquisition, is to establish that fact beyond all shadow of doubt.

Indeed, this correspondence was the immediate occasion for me to publish, sooner than I intended, my *Morgenstunden or Lectures on the Existence of God* which I had outlined a few years ago. I made mention of that occasion in the Preface to the first Part of the *Morgenstunden*; not until the second Part was the correspondence to be made known. To be sure, it had been my original intent to initiate the philosophical debate immediately, and I even received permission from Herr Jacobi to make any use I wished[1] of his letter. Yet so many considerations had to be taken into account. The substance of the issue appeared too delicate to me, the readers too unprepared, for me to introduce such a controversial investigation without preliminaries. I wished first to clarify the *issue* itself and only then to touch upon what concerns the *persons* involved; to reveal at the very start my concepts of Spinozism, of the noxious and innocuous qualities of this system, and subsequently to consider whether the one or the other person might be an adherent of that system, and in what sense they might have understood it.

All such questions as: Was Lessing a Spinozist? Did Jacobi hear the same from Lessing himself? What precisely was their state of mind when that confidence passed between them? all such questions could be put aside until we and the reader have come to an agreement on the issue as such, what, in fact, Spinozism is or is not. Hence I changed my original plan and decided to wait until the next Part to avail myself of the kind permission of my correspondent. Except that, as I now see, he has seen fit to steal a

---

[1] [= Jacobi had only said that Mendelssohn was free to make use [freien Gebrauch] of his letter, not to make any use of it [beliebigen Gebrauch], as we have it here.]

march on me. Casting all scruples aside, he throws down a bone of contention amongst the public, and for all posterity he brands as a Spinozist, an atheist, and a blasphemer our friend, *Gotthold Ephraim Lessing*, Lessing--the *editor of the Fragments, the author of Nathan*, that great and respected champion of theism and of the religion of reason. What is one to do now? Surely we ought to take up the defence of our friend? The most rigourous religious tribunal is not wont to begrudge even an indicted heretic such assistance. But I should think that we might perfectly well leave the author of *Nathan* to his own defence; even if I were a Plato or a Xenophon I would never have the temerity to make a speech in defence of *this* Socrates. *Lessing*, a *hypocrite*; the *author of Nathan*, a *blasphemer*: one would be thinking the impossible if one were to combine such contradictions; one could just as easily imagine *Lessing* and *block-head* to be one and the same! For the present, since I am after all involved in the issue and Herr Jacobi is challenging me - first in personal letters and now in public - to take on our friend's cause, let us, dear reader, examine in concert the basis for the accusation. I shall go through the indictment before your very eyes, adding to the narrative what is to be added from my side, and supplying glosses wherever I deem the like to be necessary.

As Herr Jacobi tells it, he had heard from a friend [= Elise R.] that Mendelssohn was on the point of writing about Lessing's character; he enquired to what extent Lessing's religious views were known to Mendelssohn and added: *Lessing was a Spinozist.*

"My friend Elise," he said, "understood the point perfectly well; the matter seemed to her to be of extreme importance and she wrote Mendelssohn post haste in order to let him know what I had just disclosed to her."

"Mendelssohn," he continued, "was astonished, and his first reaction was to doubt the accuracy of my assertion."

The news of my astonishment is in no way a narrating of the facts but rather a supposition on the part of the narrator [= Jacobi]. What Herr Jacobi disclosed to our mutual friend, and what she in due course passed on to me, could not possibly have given rise to any such reaction on my part. My conviction as to the un-truth of Spinozism can absolutely not be shaken, neither by Lessing's repute nor by that of any other mortal; neither could this report have the least effect on my friendship with Lessing; nor, by the same token, could my opinion of Lessing's genius and character be the lesser because of it. *Lessing, a follower of Spinoza?* Good Lord! What have a person's speculative views to do with the person himself? Who would not be delighted to have had Spinoza as friend, no matter how great his Spinozism? And who would refuse to give Spinoza's genius and excellent character their due?

As long as my friend still was not accused of being a secret blasphemer and a hypocrite to boot, the news of his being a Spinozist was a matter of complete indifference to me. I knew that there is also a refined Spinozism which rhymes very well with all that is practical in religion and morality, as demonstrated at length in my *Morgenstunden*; I knew that, in the main, this refined Spinozism can be easily reconciled with Judaism, and that Spinoza, irrespective of his speculative doctrine, could have remained an orthodox Jew were it not that in other writings he had called genuine Judaism into question and in so doing stepped outside the *Law.* Obviously Spinoza's doctrine would come much closer to Judaism than does the orthodox doctrine of the Christians. If I was able indeed to love Lessing and be loved in return where he was still a strict follower of Athanasius (or was at least considered so by me), then why not all the more where he approximated Judaism, and where I saw in him an adherent of the Jew, *Baruch Spinoza?* The label of Jew and Spinozist could be for me in no way so startling or so grating as it would seem to be for Herr Jacobi.

Finally, I had already been aware that in his earliest youth our friend had inclined to pantheism; and I knew that not only was he able to harmonize it with his religious system, but that he even sought, by means of it, to prove the Athanasian creed. A passage from a very early essay by this precocious writer, which I quote in the *Morgenstunden,* demonstrates this most clearly, and it was at the very outset of our acquaintance that he had given it to me for my perusal.

The news that Lessing was a Spinozist could in consequence neither astonish nor alienate me. But Jacobi's assertion I found most offensive; that, I must confess. After all, I had never made Herr Jacobi's acquaintance. I knew of his merits as a writer; but I had never read anything by him in the field of metaphysics. Neither did I know that he had enjoyed Lessing's friendship and personal company. Hence I took the report to be purely anecdotal, something which a visiting traveller might possibly have passed on to him. Everyone is familiar with this species of traveller in Germany, who totes an autograph album along from town to town, breathlessly retelling everywhere whatever they see of or ferret out from a man of merit, even hastening with it to the public press. Perhaps, I thought, someone like that picked up some garbled word of Lessing's or Lessing had written in his album the Greek motto: ONE AND ALL, and in a trice the monger of anecdotes made Lessing into a Spinozist. At the same time, I could well see that the intent was to convict Lessing without a hearing. The Germans have become accustomed. by studying natural history, to classifying everything. If they are at a loss as to what to make of someone's views and writings, they take the first opportunity to subsume him under a classification, making him into an "-ist," as though that settled the matter. Since I was in fact preparing to write about Lessing's character, I saw very well that this anecdote would carry me far off course, that it required discussions and investigations for which I had no heart, and that it would lead me astray into thorny subtleties and force me to rekindle a debate that should have been over long ago. Most unwelcome, then, this statement of Herr Jacobi's, and I pressed him for further clarification: how had Lessing demonstrated his Spinozism? on what occasion? with what words? The questions I put to Herr Jacobi are couched in terms somewhat too aggressive, but they are certainly appropriate to the issue; they were not said out of undue sensitivity on my part.

I received that added clarification I had requested - and in full measure. An epistle from Herr Jacobi addressed to me made it abundantly clear that I had not taken the true measure of my man; that Jacobi had penetrated the subtleties of the Spinozist doctrine more deeply than I had assumed; that he really had enjoyed Lessing's personal company; that he frequently had engaged him in intimate conversations, and that, finally, the news of Lessing's devotion to Spinoza was not to be seen as a mere retailing of anecdote but as the sum total of those same intimate conversations.

Anyone who knows such intimate conversations, anyone who has ever had the good fortune to enjoy them, would never question the sincerity and integrity of the conclusions reached in them. Within the sanctuary of friendship it is not simply a matter of mind opening itself to mind, but of heart to heart, disclosing its innermost secret folds and recesses. Friend unveils to friend all his most secret doubts, weaknesses, shortcomings, and flaws, that a kindly hand may touch, perhaps even heal them. Anyone who never tasted the bliss of such an hour of the heart's outpouring has never really known joy. But think for a moment of poor *Rousseau* when he, yearning with all his heart for that soul's balm, comes up instead against a granite-like soul that rejects him with all its strength!

Had this been the nature of the conversations Jacobi conducted with Lessing, then we would certainly have nothing to propose to exculpate our friend; we would have to accept the fact that Lessing was the most enigmatic character who ever lived, a peculiar combination of duplicity and arrogance; on the one hand, inflexibly close-mouthed; on the other, open to the point of childish frivolity. But if this were so, I should be sincerely sorry: for myself, for my friend Lessing, and for Herr Jacobi as well.

For myself: I must confess, it would humble me greatly, had our friend Lessing deemed me, who so loved him and was so loved by him, to be unworthy of the confidence that another mortal was able to gain on such short acquaintance, and this after I had lived with him in intimate friendship for over thirty years, had unceasingly sought with him the truth, had conversed with him repeatedly, by letter and face to face, on those important matters. I confess my frailty. There is no creature on earth I would not begrudge such preferment.

For my friend Lessing: how he must have been failing those last days of his life, if he did say in complete and heart-felt confidence all that he is reported to have said in that conversation. In that conversation he does not appear as the bold, resolute thinker who follows his reason and by that reason is led astray; there, he is a shallow-minded atheist, not a disciple of a Hobbes or a Spinoza but of some childish jokester who takes pleasure in booting aside anything his fellow man holds important and dear.

To be sure, Herr Jacobi admits to having abbreviated and summarized the conversations. Nevertheless, his well-known rectitude should permit us to assume that the chiefest point at issue has not suffered in the process, and that he has attributed to each person what each actually did. But in all that Lessing proposes there, not one single solitary thought can be found that is sane. All the reasonable arguments redound to Herr Jacobi's credit. He defends Spinozism with all the cleverness the system allows. Lessing does not offer even the slightest counter-proposition of any import; he accepts as correct and persuasive the very arguments the two of us had so often reflected upon in past conversations and had judged on their true merits; only from time to time does he interrupt his friend with an eccentric idea that as often as not is tantamount to blasphemy. Could Lessing, in a sincere, intimate outpouring of his heart, forget himself to such a degree?

And then to top it all: Lessing's evaluation of the *Prometheus* poem which Jacobi put in his hands, and was able to do so only because of the boldness of its content, certainly not because of any excellence in it; and Lessing found it so good! Thou wretched judge of art! how low must you have fallen that you find this paltry thing in earnest good! On his better days, I frequently saw him hand back to some poet much more acceptable verses, saying: "Not bad, my friend, not bad! but why in verses? Why don't you first see whether you would like these ideas in prose!" Herr Jacobi was reluctant to include those verses in his book without a disclaiming device: he enclosed a blank and blameless piece of paper which readers of tender conscience could insert between the pages in lieu of the corrupting verses. As I knew him, Lessing would have found the admonition more harmful than the poison. Anyone who can lose his religion because of bad verse surely has little to lose. In a word: if the dialogue is supposed to represent serious, intimate confidence, then I fail totally to discern the stamp of Lessing's character in anything he contributes; I miss his acumen, I miss his humour, I miss his philosophy, and I miss his critical sense.

But *for Herr Jacobi* as well, I would sincerely regret it if he were to take the conversation with Lessing as a confidence, proffered him by our friend. All of Herr Jacobi's friends and acquaintances praise his rectitude, valuing his heart even more than they do his intellectual gifts. But how can his behaviour toward Lessing be reconciled with such rectitude as this? A friend entrusts a confession to his ear, and he betrays it to the public; a friend, as his life is drawing to a close, makes him the confidant of his frailty, and this he uses to stain the man's memory for all posterity. In the end he has indicted his friend without being able to cite any witness to the offence other than his own person. "His own person": by admitting complicity, by admitting that he had even played the greater role in the affair, that it was less a case of having found Lessing on the paths of error than of having himself led his friend onto those paths. Ultimately, he is cautious enough to keep open an escape route by which he manages to avoid atheism and to return to the shelter of faith. But why does he block the path behind him, denying his poor accomplice a like opportunity to slip away? Why must his friend be left behind, a poor defenseless victim? I repeat yet again: if Jacobi really believed that Lessing entrusted him with a secret he wished kept, his behaviour would be irresponsible.

But even more inexplicable would I find his behaviour towards me. In the introduction to his essay he relates that Lessing gave him to understand that he esteemed me most among his friends; Jacobi, for his part, in the course of a philosophical discussion with Lessing, expressed his surprise that a person such as I could have accepted the proof of God's existence from its idea, with the fervour I show in my treatise on evidence; Lessing's *excuses*, Jacobi continues, led him directly to ask "whether he had ever propounded his own system to Mendelssohn." - "Never," Lessing answered .... "Once I did speak to him about approximately the same things that caught your attention in *The Education of the Human Race* (§73). We could not reach any agreement and I left it at that."

So then: Lessing was tolerant of my weakness; he excused *a priori* my fervour in metaphysical argumentation, concealed his real system from me - his most esteemed friend - apparently in order not to rob me of a conviction in which he saw me so cosily ensconsed. These are the words Herr Jacobi heard from Lessing's own mouth at exactly the same time he was being made privy to Lessing's great secret. And all of this notwithstanding, I am the very first person Jacobi seeks out, to press this dangerous secret upon, the secret my friend had so considerately sought to spare me. If all these events occurred exactly as they appear to have occurred, then let me pose this one question: Who has exhibited here more of *practical* religion, of truer piety - the atheist who is unwilling to rob his friend of his conviction as to natural religion, a conviction in which he saw him content, or the orthodox Christian who, so to speak, without mercy knocks from the cripple's hands the crutches with which he just barely manages to drive himself along?

There is only one single way I can imagine how all this happened, a way which will remove all these perplexities and apparent contradictions; and though it be merely my own hypothesis, it nevertheless appears to me, in view of Herr Jacobi's manifest aim, the most natural one and commensurate with the character of the persons involved.

"The intent of my work," says Herr Jacobi in his Preface, "is stated concisely after the last letter contained in it; and it is quite clearly expressed in that final section, I should think." Verily, nothing can be clearer, and it is well meant and sincere, that intent. Herr Jacobi obviously purposes to lead his fellow-men, who have lost their way in the arid wastes of speculation, back to the straight and narrow path of *faith*. All his talks with Lessing, all his correspondence with Hemsterhuis, with our friend Elise, and with me, point in that one direction.

First of all, concerning Lessing: perhaps Jacobi did not himself believe that Lessing had entrusted him with a special secret but took Lessing instead for a man of unsound principles who had a talent for asserting with the same quick-wittedness first one thing and then another, to-day theism and to-morrow a cheap kind of atheism, and perhaps some superstitious fad the day after; a man who never makes a secret of his opinion, never hesitating to announce it to all and sundry as the mood or spirit of contradiction prompts him. He took Lessing for an errant sophist, hopelessly lost in his own subtleties, who sees truth and error in the same light or in the same darkness; a person who ultimately prizes wit as much as philosophy; and who, if he is so disposed, seems to regard blasphemy as evidence of strength of mind.

Jacobi believed he had found our friend in just this deplorable state of mental confusion, and magnanimously resolved to cure him of his ills. Like a skillful physician he took the risk of first aggravating the illness so as to be able later to cure it the more effectively. He led Lessing deeper and deeper into the labyrinths of Spinozism and lured him into the thorny thickets of pantheism in order to make all the more tempting the sole means of exit he would in the fulness of time reveal to him. The way out, as we now see clearly enough, was to retreat to the shelter of faith. Jacobi tried to convince Lessing that, as he puts it, certain things cannot be explained; that, nevertheless, one ought not to ignore them but accept them as they are; and that one must of necessity draw back from philosophy, which inevitably leads to total scepticism. When Lessing, made curious, asks: "Where do you go from there?" the answer is given: "You follow the light which, Spinoza says, illumines both itself and the darkness"; thus the Spinoza who had caused Lessing to stray so far was now to help him back onto the path to truth.

Our friend, who in all likelihood soon sensed the sincerity of Herr Jacobi's intentions, was roguish enough to reinforce Jacobi's view of him. He may, in part, have enjoyed the keen wit with which Jacobi could present and vindicate Spinoza's doctrine. You know that our friend took greater pleasure in hearing an absurd proposition cleverly argued than in hearing the truth poorly defended. Hence he played the attentive pupil perfectly, never contradicting, agreeing with everything; and whenever the discussion threatened to come to a halt, he would seek to revive it with some witticism. This is why I, albeit his most intimate friend, was to know naught of that great secret, and that even Gleim could not participate in that metaphysical charade. That generous, jove-like host, no stranger to his visitors' philosophy and whimsy, would soon have put an end to the *badinage*. This, the reason finally for the banalities and the tortured metaphors, for the pleasure found in bad verse - all most unnatural in a Lessing.

Be that as it may - I will pursue my hypothesis, for it seems increasingly plausible to me. Jacobi, realizing that his experiment with Lessing was going awry and motivated still by the same pious intent, believed that he had to make an edifying example of Lessing as a warning to all other witlings so that they could make timely use of the medication essential for any hope of recovery. Let them betimes learn to pursue the light that illumines even the surrounding darkness, unless they mean to follow Lessing, Leibniz, Wolff, and all the other metaphysical quibblers in becoming determinists and consequently, as Jacobi would have it, fatalists, Spinozists - and hence *atheists* - unless they intend to abandon themselves to extremest scepticism! "Every proof," as he puts it [in his third presentation of Spinozism], "presupposes something already proven, the first principle of which is revelation"; and again: "The prime element of all human knowledge and action is faith."

Since Herr Jacobi is not acquainted with me personally, I too may have been described to him as a witling, someone who concedes too much to reason and to faith nothing at all; someone who labours under the illusion that he can accomplish anything with the aid of metaphysical demonstrations (e.g., that with his quiddities he can exorcise spirits or combat the machinations of a certain secret society). Hence Jacobi's earnest endeavour to cure me too of my illness, if at all possible; hence the right he usurps to reveal to me the secret our friend so assiduously intended to hide from me. That good and honest intent to guide me to the bosom of faith, though not justifying everything, can at least excuse a great deal.

Right from the start I had suspected something of the sort, having often experienced such well-intentioned attempts on the part of some of my contemporaries [= e.g., Lavater]. In my reply [= *Comments*] therefore, I gave Herr Jacobi to understand that in my case the cure was doomed to failure and that, in respect of doctrines and eternal truths, I recognized no conviction save that grounded in reason. Judaism demands a faith in historical truths, in *facts* upon which the authority of our prescribed [positiv] ritual law is founded. The existence and authority of the Supreme Law-giver, however, must be recognized by reason, and there is no room here for revelation or faith, neither according to the principles of Judaism nor my own. Further, Judaism is not revealed *religion* but revealed *law*. As a Jew, I said, I had even more reason to seek conviction through rational arguments.

Permit me to speak further to the statement just quoted, which otherwise might too easily be misinterpreted. My assertion that Judaism in no wise presumes belief in eternal truths but simply historical belief, is clearly set forth in a more appropriate place to which I refer the reader [*Jerusalem, oder über religiöse Macht und Judentum* (1783)]. The Hebrew language has no proper word for what we call *religion*. Neither is Judaism a revelation of doctrinal statements and eternal truths which demanded our belief. It consists exclusively of revealed laws of worship and presumes a natural and reasonable conviction as to religious truths, without which no divine law can be established. But when I speak of reasonable conviction and insist on making it an incontestable premise within Judaism, I am not speaking of the metaphysical argumentation we usually carry out in books; nor am I speaking of

scholastic demonstrations that withstand every test to which the
subtlest of doubts may subject them; but I speak of the statements
and judgments of a simple, sound, common sense
[Menschenverstand] which looks things directly in the eye and
reflects upon them calmly. To be sure, I am a great admirer of
metaphysical demonstrations and am convinced that the main truths
of natural religion are as demonstrable apodictically as can be any
theorem of geometry. Yet even *my* conviction about religious truths
is not so totally dependent on metaphysical arguments that it would
be doomed to stand and fall with them. Doubts can be raised
against my arguments, errors of inference pointed out, yet will my
conviction remain unshakable. Petrus Ramus [= Pierre La Ramée,
1515-1572, a logician], who could raise a whole host of doubts
against Euclid's axioms and postulates, still remained totally
convinced of the truth of Euclidian principles. Any number of
mathematicians can question the evidence of Euclid's axiom of the
parallel lines and yet stake happiness and life on the truth and
irrefutability of the postulates derived from it. Now, it seems to
me, the evidence of natural religion is just as obvious, just as
irrefutably certain to an uncorrupted, untraduced human
understanding as is any theorem of geometry. At every stage of
life, at every level of enlightenment, one has talents and ability
enough, sufficient opportunity and power to become convinced of
the truths of the religion of reason. The reasoning of the
Greenlander who, walking on the ice sheet with a missionary one
fine morning, saw the sun's rays bursting forth among the icebergs
and said to the Moravian missionary: "Behold, my friend, the new
day! How beautiful must he be who made that!" that argument, so
convincing to the Greenlander before the Moravian corrupted his
understanding, I still find convincing; it has for me the same power
as the plain, artless reasoning of the Psalmist:

> Shall he who implanted the ear not hear,
> he who fashioned the eye not see?
> [...]
> Yahweh, the teacher of all people,
> knows human plans [...].
>   (Psalm 94:9-11)

This natural conclusion that even a child could draw, retains for
me the authority of a geometric axiom or postulate; it has the
triumphant force of an irrefutable proof. I assign to speculation

merely the business of rectifying the statements of sound common sense and of transforming them, as far as possible, into rational knowledge. As long as the two - sound reason and speculative thought - are on good terms, I will follow them wherever they may lead. Whenever they part company, I try to re-orient myself and bring them both back, if at all possible, to our point of departure. Since superstition, priestly wiles, contrariness, and sophistry have warped our vision and confused our sound common sense with all manner of hair-splittings and sleight-of-hand, we must of course employ our own devices to come to its aid. We must measure against truth those metaphysical subtleties used to deceive us, compare them and test them, and if they do not stand the test, seek to replace them with yet more refined concepts. Such artificial methods are hardly as necessary to true, genuine conviction as to natural religion, to the kind of conviction that may impinge upon man's happiness. Any human being, whose reason is unspoiled by sophistry, needs but follow his sense of what is right and happiness is assured. I shall deal with this in more detail in the sequel to my *Morgenstunden*; I shall content myself here with a quotation from a philosopher whose two little books [= C.H. Müller, *Der Dorfprediger* and *Die Dorfschule* (1785)] are very worthwhile reading and, though showing much dissatisfaction with philosophy, contain much that is sound philosophy:

"Natural religion is both the simplest religion and the one that is most intelligible; it is so accessible, so geared to the capacities of Everyman that one can only be amazed when philosophers are heard to say in earnest that it is not meant for common folk. On many an occasion I have attempted to explain to some peasant the natural ideas concerning the Supreme Being; in each instance the fellow grasped it quickly, digested the information, and drew proper conclusions. He felt the force of those ideas; they cheered, comforted, strengthened his soul. Those ideas are related to all that is beautiful, good, and perfect among human beings; they illumine all those qualities and draw benefit from them; the one makes the other almost tangible, the one reinforces the other.

"When I compare the lucidity of the concepts found in natural religion with the obscurity of the concepts put forward by revealed religion, and then have to listen to people who tell me that the common folk can understand the latter but not the former [= my revised punctuation: der gemeine Mann könne die letzten, nicht aber die ersten verstehen]: then my mind is at a loss, etc."

I return now from this digression to my objections to Herr Jacobi. Here are the *Comments* concerning his conversations with Lessing which I sent him at the time and to which the rest of his work is related.

[= At this point the text of the *Comments* is reproduced as found above]

Subsequently, I received Herr Jacobi's reply dated September 5th, 1784, a "copie d'une lettre à Monsieur Hemsterhuis," and lastly a correspondence in German dated April 21st, 1785, in response to the *Comments* I had sent him. There is no further mention of Lessing in these letters. Determining on his own the future course of the debate, Herr Jacobi tries to convince both Herr Hemsterhuis and me that speculative reason, when consistent, leads perforce to Spinozism; he tries to persuade us that, once someone has reached the precipitous peaks of metaphysics, there is no recourse but to turn one's back on all philosophy and plunge head first into the depths of faith.

In my *Morgenstunden* I have already expressed my views on Spinozism itself and on what can bring a person to it; what I have to say specifically about Herr Jacobi's manner of defending that doctrine, I shall reserve for another occasion. At this point, the public merely has to decide between Jacobi and Lessing, and, in effect, between Jacobi and me as well. And since a referee must have at hand everything pertinent to the matter under debate, let the Introduction of Jacobi's essay from April 1785 be reproduced here [= not translated in the present book]. Herr Jacobi omitted it, he says, because it only contains the reasons why he "deemed it good to contrast Mendelssohn's *Comments* simply with a new presentation of Spinoza, focusing on the justification of my understanding of that system."

(...)

Abraham de Moivre [= 1667-1754, British mathematician of French descent] is said once to have asked Newton to provide him with the proof for a mathematical theorem he himself could not locate. Newton was happy to comply with the request; but the proof's premises were even more difficult for de Moivre to understand than the theorem itself; the more explanation Newton was at pains to provide, the less Moivre was able to comprehend it. Almost the same thing transpired between me and Herr Jacobi. The more important he thought it was to assume the burden of enlightening me as to the true, authentic Spinozism, the less I understood - either him or his Spinoza. I literally did not understand them. You may call me a shallow thinker or a *half-wit*; I simply do not understand a language that is too transcendental one moment, and too metaphorical the next. I find lacking at every turn a clear explanation of the terms or definition of the concepts; everything is wavering before my eyes like vague shapes seen at twilight. It was impossile to decide whether certain statements, whose words I thought I understood, were to be taken as being *pro* or *contra*; rather, it appeared that the same reasons could be used to argue either way; so many other assertions seemed so obviously untenable that I could not believe I had properly grasped their true meaning. I had then to question whether, as Herr Jacobi expresses it, I had even engaged my opponent at all and was in any position to do combat with him. Let me give a few examples. In his letter to Hemsterhuis, Herr Jacobi has his Spinoza prove that the will cannot produce any transformation in nature and puts the following words in his mouth: "La pensée considérée dans son essence n'est que le sentiment de l'Etre. L'idée est le sentiment de l'Etre, en tant qu'il est déterminé individuel et en relation avec d'autres individus. La volonté n'est que le sentiment de l'Etre déterminé agissant comme individu." Now, because the word *être* is ambiguous in French, let us look at the translation Herr Jacobi himself appended: "Thinking, considered in its essence, is none other than *Being that feels itself.*" I must confess that this a sentence I simply do not understand. The word "thinking" is far clearer to me than the words: "Being that feels itself." Is this to mean, "Thinking, considered in its essence, is nothing but the self-consciousness that one exists?" This seems to be the case, if I compare it with the same idea Herr Jacobi presents me with; for his letter to me, in German, reads: "Absolute thinking is the pure, immediate, absolute consciousness in universal Being, in the Being *kat' exochen* or in the Substance." But here too, I only half understand these ideas; for I still cannot grasp what *universal Being, Being par excellence, or Substance* are supposed to mean. In a note, Herr Jacobi says: "The expression 'le sentiment Etre,' which

French provided me with in my letter to Hemsterhuis, was purer and better; for the word 'consciousness' seems to imply something of representation and reflection, which is not the case here." And to explain his idea more closely, he quotes a passage from the *Critique of Pure Reason.* For *Kant,* however, some form of consciousness is merely *at the root* of every concept - while for Jacobi thinking is supposed *to be nothing but consciousness*: these are two totally separate and distinct positions. Further, it seems to me that Spinoza must admit that there are representations without consciousness, if he wants to be consistent; for since, according to his doctrine, everything that occurs in the body through movement is harmoniously expressed in the soul through representation; and since it cannot be denied that movements occur within the body of which we are not aware, then there must of necessity exist obscure, dormant representations without any consciousness. Therefore, to follow Spinoza, concepts without consciousness, or a *thinking without the Being that feels itself,* must be entirely possible. What Jacobi says of the will is totally incomprehensible to me: "The will is nothing but Being that feels itself insofar as it is determined and acts as individual being." Here I am at a loss to understand the literal sense of the words, nor can I understand the explanation of thinking which he repeats: "Thinking," he writes, "is Being that feels itself. Consequently, everything that occurs in the extension must equally occur in thinking; and every individual *qua individual* is animated according to the *measure of its manifoldness and unity,* or according to the degree of the power by virtue of which it is what it is." What is *the essence of man himself, or the basis of his real capacity, or of the power by virtue of which he is what he is*? Never in the world would it have occurred to me to look for the *freedom of the will* behind those transcendental terms through which Spinoza attempts to explain it only to contest it in his own way. I could not possibly think of discussing those arguments since I did not understand the meaning of the words.

Spinoza, Herr Jacobi says, considered the system of final causes to be the greatest aberration of human understanding; he even goes so far as to have Spinoza say that the doctrine of finality is arrant nonsense. If he meant that in all seriousness, then it strikes me as the most insolent statement that ever fell from mortal lips. A statement like that ought never to be uttered by any child of this earth, who no more than we feeds on ambrosia, who has had to eat our common bread, to sleep, and to perish along with all the rest of humankind. If a philosopher in his musings formulates a claim so monstrous, then it is high time, it seems to me, that he re-orient himself and search for the simple human understanding which he has left so far behind.

Indeed, according to Herr Jacobi, Spinoza is not about to be refuted by experience. "We can also see," he says, "that the sun circles the earth. But let us put appearances [Erscheinungen] aside and try to know things as they are." In cases such as this, however, what appears to the senses cannot simply be set aside. Its testimony is, on the contrary, of the greatest validity: viewed as that which appears, it speaks pure truth. It is also true that the sun circles the earth, if we look only at the inhabitants of the earth and do not draw the conclusion that it has to appear the same to inhabitants of other planets. Are there such things as intentions and final causes in nature? If such are found in the human being, if he has them and does carry them out, and if they are carried out by dint of his powers, constituent parts, and limbs, then we cannot gainsay nature those same final causes. Herr Jacobi tries to brush aside final causes in the universe by using the following ratiocination: "Let us consider the intricate organization of the bodies politic and discover what makes them into a whole; the more one ruminates upon it, the more one perceives only blind motives and the machinistic method of their operation - a machine, to be sure, like those primary, self-organizing ones in which forces come into play according to their own requirements and the degree of their energy; a machine in which all the coil-springs sense their own effects, a sensation they communicate to one another through mutual impulses in a necessarily unending series of motions. The same applies to languages, whose overall structure seems a miraculous thing, though not one language ever came into being with the help of grammatical rules." And this, therefore, the splendid insight Spinoza opposes to the plain, commonly accepted system of final causes; these, the compelling reasons with which he makes bold to accuse us of folly and madness! Well now: people with a common need can constitute a reasonable body politic without prior negotiations; people who are trying to make themselves understood, can, without grammar, create an intelligible, even a quite respectable language; and even things devoid of knowledge and intent can collide and spontaneously bring forth the wonders of the great universe, just as La Mettrie's painter brought forth the foam at the mouth of his steed. Anyone who does not understand that, is not in his right mind and the whole human race is not in its right mind if it fails to grasp this simple reasoning. Are we to believe that anybody has ever made these claims in all seriousness?

No fact, it seems to me, can be more incontrovertible than the fact that, in the visible world around us and in the world within us, *final causes* are aimed at and *intentions* are carried out. It is impossible for me to believe that there ever was a philosopher who cast serious doubts upon that fact. We need but open our eyes, consider any work of nature with a minimum of attention, to be utterly convinced of it. The question that arises in metaphysics and is worth considering, is, properly stated:

> Whether or not the system of final causes can be demonstrated apodictically? i.e., whether a single fact is sufficient to lead us *scientifically* to the conclusion that a final cause obtains, or whether, rather, a number of individual cases right up to evident *induction* must be accumulated in order for us to be convinced of it?

The solution to that problem has no special impact upon either religion or morality. As far as the consequences are concerned, it makes little difference whether we are convinced of a truth *apodictically* or by way of *evident induction*. But such an investigation has its useful and pleasant sides for the speculative turn of mind, and it ought to be undertaken with all due keenness and precision of mind. But that a man like Spinoza declares out of hand the system of final causes to be insane, mad; that he relegates to the level of numbskulls all of us who are firm subscribers to that system: that is quite a provocative insult which the system's champion attempts to excuse by appealing to the chivalrous custom and to the tradition of philosophical dispute.

For some time I did not respond to Jacobi's letter to Hemsterhuis which Herr Jacobi had sent to me. Basically there was nothing to which I could respond. As a matter of fact, his letter had not been addressed to me; I did not understand it, putting the blame partly on my poor knowledge of the French language, and I intended to wait for the response in German to my *Comments* which Herr Jacobi had promised. Since his reply was taking too long for my taste, I decided to publish my *Morgenstunden*, in the meantime written in their entirety, and had a request sent to Herr Jacobi to delay his counter-comments until he had the first Part of the *Morgenstunden* in his hands. In that request I stated expressly that no mention of our correspondence was made in the first Part of my work. My intent there was merely to articulate ideas on the *first grounds of knowledge*, on *truth*, *illusion*, and *error*, and to attempt to apply them to pantheism. Herr Jacobi, I thought, will perhaps find here the point at which we can convene and from which we can depart so as to bring our contest to an end. This was to take place in my Second Part.

But when, immediately thereafter, I received Herr Jacobi's letter and his *presentation of Spinozism* written in German, I was forced to abandon any hope of ever reaching an agreement with that philosopher on even one point. If Spinoza in French was beyond my grasp, Spinoza in German was totally enshrouded in fog and cloud. I couldn't grasp one single thought of his; the moment I dared try, I had to drop it when reading the next sentence. At times it seemed to me as though, according to Spinoza, all changeable things were mere ideas and representations of the unchangeable; but at other times he seemed to ascribe objective existence to the changeable as well: though all the time he was asserting that the infinite is not an aggregate of finite elements, that in no way can a higher degree be obtained by the accumulating of smaller degrees, and that therefore *an infinite manifold cannot constitute an infinite*. Unscathed by all this, the changeable was supposed nonetheless to be *one* with and the same substance as the unchangeable. Then again, at another time I derived from his words that his infinite is a mere *abstractum quid*, a general concept, which is eternal, infinite and unchangeable solely because it is to be encountered in everything finite and changeable and to function as its basis. As a result, only the finite would have concrete existence, but the infinite would be a concept which can be distinguished from the finite. *Absolute unity* itself, which he ascribes to his one and only possible substance, seemed in several passages to be a mere *unity of abstraction* as, for instance, "in concept," *animality* in all animals, or *humanity* in all humans, is *one* - whereas "in reality" it belongs separately to each and every individual. It is the same force of gravity that moves the heavenly bodies above and the pendulum of the clock here below. "In concept" therefore, it is all *one and the same force*; but "in reality" this force has to be repeated and multiplied in each actual individual thing if it is to produce so many transformations. It seemed to me that Spinoza's *unity* had to be understood only "in concept" because that in which all that is changeable meets is, "in concept," *one* and always *the same thing*, although "in reality" it is repeated in each individual thing. But yet again, I could not reconcile this train of thought with other passages. In a word, I was as if whirled round and round in circles and nowhere could I stand steadily on my feet. I understood then the necessity of having several disputants and arbitrators take part in our military-like manoeuvres and wrote our mutual friend Elise the following letter on May 24th, 1785.

"Here you have, [dearest Elise], the portion of my manuscript which I have decided to publish. Be so kind as to show it to [your brother] for his critical evaluation. I have no philosopher friend who can surpass him in outspokenness, love of truth, and critical judgment, who has more good-will and a greater ability to tell me the truth about this work of mine. Implore him, my dearest friend, to devote a few of his free hours to me and return the manuscript as soon as is convenient along with corrections from his own hand. I shall send the sequel before long. I cannot let Herr Jacobi see this manuscript; he is to see the whole work in printed form; the reason for this, you will hear straight away.

"My relationship with Herr Jacobi has taken an odd turn. The more he attempts to explain, the less I understand him. I literally did not understand his letter to Hemsterhuis; and now, a few days ago, I received a elaborate dissertation from him that was to serve as an explanation of that letter and also as a response to my *Comments* on his interpretation, and - I do not blush to admit it- I understand his latest effort still less. Now what am I to do? If we speak in different idioms and do not understand each other, then in all eternity we will never get out of each other's hair. Then too, Herr Jacobi seems now and then to become agressive, falling into a kind of fury; although this may well be feigned merely to enliven the controversy. Actually, there is still a chance that in his heart he is free of all self-conceit and self-righteousness.

"Be that as it may, in order to avoid misunderstandings, I must first set out my principles before joining issue with Herr Jacobi. I shall therefore publish the first Part of my *Morgenstunden, without making any reference to our whole correspondence*; yet I shall touch upon Spinozism and seek to refute it. *I reserve our correspondence for the second Part which is to appear a year later.* Perhaps I will come to understand Herr Jacobi better in the meantime, or be so fortunate as to reach agreement with him on a few points. Before we start our race, we must meet at some starting-line."

The unprejudiced reader will have to decide for himself whether Herr Jacobi's concern was justified after all that occurred between us, and judge if he had the right to rush private letters into print without leave of the correspondents involved. "I could really not," he says, "leave it up to him, unilaterally, to give the debate its proper introduction and to show publicly the reasons why many points (in my essays) strike him as being absolutely incomprehensible, constantly evading his perception, the more explanations I try to give him. Still less," he continues, "could I permit a *status controversiae* to be established in which it would fall to me, so to speak, to play the *advocatus diaboli*, unless at the same time the whole occasion for the controversy was to be made public at the outset. It was extremely important to me that it be perfectly clear in what sense I had taken Spinoza's part, and that it had been purely and simply a case of one speculative philosophy against another speculative philosophy, or more correctly, of pure metaphysics against pure metaphysics." As Herr Jacobi himself mentions, he already had in his hands my assurance of May 26th that I would make absolutely no mention of our correspondence in the first Part of my work; that consequently, I was in no way going to mention Herr Jacobi's essays and their comprehensibility or lack thereof. If, as may be assumed, our friend Elise sent him a copy of my letter dated May 24th [= Jacobi never saw that letter], then he will have found there the reiterated promise that our dispute would not appear until the second Part, and I could not, without being blatantly two-faced, act counter to that promise. Now my *Morgenstunden* have appeared and it is evident that nothing of what Herr Jacobi feared has happened. Where did I say that I intend to show *publicly* the reasons why many points in his essays strike me as being absolutely incomprehensible, etc.? Herr Jacobi himself quotes me as saying only: "*At least the reasons will become apparent why* etc.," that is, once I have established in my own way, in the first Part of my work, the *status controversiae* with pantheism in general, it would soon be quite clear to the two of us for what reasons.... But how correctly or incorrectly I would represent the *status controversiae*, Herr Jacobi could have waited to see without running any risks of personal injury. It was still a matter of pantheism in general, not of Herr Jacobi in particular, who, had he caught me on crooked paths, would still have had time to set me and the public aright without being unduly hasty in divulging private correspondence. Still less could Herr Jacobi be apprehensive that I might picture him as an adherent of atheism. Even if I had not promised to eschew mention of our debate, I still had given him no occasion for such unworthy suspicion. What could ever move me to deprive of his good reputation for all time a person who had never given me offence? Herr Jacobi will certainly not stand in my way on the course I am taking through this world and whose end I have now almost reached. If he really thought me capable of malicious joy in tripping up an innocent person simply to amuse myself at his fall, then he should have sought neither my correspondence nor my company.

But then, if it is so important, as Herr Jacobi thinks, whether and in what way one sides with Spinoza and tries to defend that philosopher's doctrines, why does he make bold to present our friend Lessing as the devil's advocate (to use his own words), to slander a deceased person who can no longer defend himself and against whom the only evidence he is able to produce is oral, the only witness, his own person?

In a word, I can make as little sense of Herr Jacobi's practical principles as I can of his theoretical ones. Circumstances being what they are, little can be accomplished by discussion, I believe, and the best course to follow is to part company. Let him return to the faith of his fathers, submit restive reason to the triumphant authority of faith, crush rising doubts with authoritative and mighty dicta, as he does in the epilogue to his work, *pronounce a benediction* over his child-like return with words from the "pious and angelic" lips of Lavater.

I for my part continue in my Jewish unbelief, ascribe *pious and angelic* lips to no mortal. When we are speaking of eternal truths on which man's happiness is founded, I eschew any desire to depend on the authority of even an *archangel*; here either I must fall or I must stand on my own two feet. Or better still, since "we are all of us born within faith," as Herr Jacobi says, I too shall return to the faith of my fathers, which, according to the original meaning of the [= Hebrew] word, is constituted not by belief in any doctrine or opinion, but by trust in and reliance on the attributes of God. I have complete, unlimited trust in God's omnipotence: His omnipotence *has been able* to give humankind the power to recognize the truths upon which its happiness rests; I harbour the child-like trust in His infinite mercy, that it *intended* to invest me with those powers. Strengthened by that unwavering faith, I seek instruction and conviction wherever I find them. Praise be to the glorious benevolence of my Creator! I *believe* I have found it and *believe* anyone can find it who seeks with open eyes and does not himself block that light. This is where matters stand, as far as I am concerned.

As regards our friend Lessing, his lot does not turn out to be as harsh as one might have expected from the outset. Herr Jacobi places him in a company which might not displease him that much. According to a paper he quotes above, Herr Jacobi does indeed declare that "Spinozism is atheism"; nevertheless, in his eyes, the philosophy of a Leibniz or a Wolff is no less fatalistic than the philosophy of Spinoza and, as he puts it, must inevitably reconduct the inveterate scholar back to Spinoza's principles. Finally, he adds, "all ways of demonstration end in fatalism." The spirit of Lessing, who used to derive such pleasure from the company of those outcasts, will hardly fear boredom in their company now. Let him then return appeased and at peace, to the embrace of his companions who trod the path of demonstration as did he and who also, as did he, placed some confidence in their own reason.

H. Jacobi, *Wider Mendelssohns Beschuldigungen in dessen Schreiben an die Freunde Lessings.* Leipzig 1786; *Werke* IV, 2, Leipzig 1819.

[From Scholz, *Hauptschriften*, pp. 332, 334-341, 345-351, 358-360, 362-364]

[From the Foreword]

... It may well be that, after the publication of this work, the tumult will redouble from one side while just beginning in earnest on the other; but yet a calm will eventually ensue. What will follow upon that calm, that I know with inmost certainty.

Meanwhile I let my "ostrich-egg" lie peacefully in the sand; titmice and magpies will hardly crush it underfoot; grackles and crows will neither hack it open nor steal it away: let the revelation of its content be entrusted to that light which rules the day.

———————————

By publishing the *Fragments* and by writing *Nathan* Lessing[1] took a public stand as a champion of theism.

"To whom but to Lessing, the defender of the Fragmentist, should the truths of the religion of reason be more inviolable (Herr Mendelssohn has his friend D. say)?... With his defence of the Fragmentist Lessing seems to have assumed also the full measure of his vision. Certainly, it is evident even in his earliest writings that, for him, the reasonable truths of religion and morality were ever holy and inviolable; but after Lessing's encounter with the Fragmentist one can detect in his writings, in all the essays written in defence of his friend or "guest", as he calls him, the same quiet conviction so typical of the Fragmentist, the same ingenuous absence of morbid doubt, the same straight course of sound human reason where the truths of the religion of reason are concerned."

I should like to respond as Lessing himself once did: "A pastor is one thing; a book-man is something else.... It is mine to make known the unknown..., one day the very Christian work of Berengarius; the next, the very un-Christian *Fragments*; and in

———————————————————————————————

[1] The present essay originally contained a personal and a factual account. We have omitted the personal, subjective part and proceed immediately to the factual account. (Scholz)

doing this it is of no concern to me if anyone feels that what I do is important or not, if it profits the one or harms the other. The concepts 'useful' and 'pernicious' are relative like 'big' or 'small.'"

But Lessing came to the defence of the Fragmentist "and seems, in so doing, to have assumed also the full measure of his vision."

That is what I do not quite understand. On the preceding page we read: "Because of the Fragmentist's great zeal for natural religion he would allow no revealed religion to stand beside it." Should we infer Lessing's devotedness to natural religion merely from the ardour he showed against any revealed one? Simply *infer* it! infer then *just like that*! The same devotedness could then be ascribed even to Spinoza; after all, in his *Tractatus theologico-politicus*, he constructed against any revealed religion a much more important monument to his fervour than did Lessing who carefully preserved all the religious terms and expressions and never rejected the label "Christian". But if we may not infer Lessing's devotedness to natural religion in that way, how on earth are we to prove it? Where can you show me one *single* passage in his work, let alone an entire essay or a book of his, that is attempting to present the truths of theism? I know how intently I looked for such things each time something by Lessing appeared, after his *Leibniz über die ewigen Strafen* and his *Wissowatius* directed my eager attention to that point. My attention was still more alerted when the philosophical essays by the young Jerusalem [= K.W. Jerusalem 1747-1772] appeared and I saw Lessing conclude his appendix to the essay on freedom with the words: "From the perspective of morality then, this system (of an absolute necessity in human actions) is unassailable. But can speculative thought not make objections of a quite different sort? Objections such as could be dealt with only by an alternative system that is equally alienating to the unsophisticated mind? That is what so often prolonged our conversation and cannot be condensed here into a few words."- Enough; I looked in vain for what could have given me a satisfactory explanation for Lessing's own system. I found theism everywhere presupposed but never professed, I found a total absence of any significant assent to it, of any decisive word in favour of its tenets. Everything concerning theism was stated in terms that could not have been more vague, more indecisive. "Quite right!" replied D. or Mendelssohn, "that is the result of his quiet conviction; of his ingenuous absence of morbid doubt; of the straight course of his sound common sense where the truth of the religion of reason is concerned." O, these clever word managers! O, these wisemen sans deceit or hypocrisy!

But what can we say of *Nathan*? *Nathan*! "this *Anti-Candide*; this glorious paean of praise of Providence, full of the felicitous attempt at justifying God's ways to man!... Where is there propounded with more conviction and accuracy of detail, with more fervent passion and pious enthusiasm the doctrine of God's providence and governance, etc.?"

Herr Mendelssohn can never quote this *Nathan* too often; I cannot help thinking finally of that famous Englishman (the Duke of Marlborough) who, in response to Burnet, referred to an event in the history of his country unknown to all and in the end came up with the *irrefutable* authority of--Shakespeare. Even a Voltaire could very well be eulogized as a zealot and a witness for the Christian religion because of his *Alzire* and *Zaïre*, if we apply a logic of this kind.

Yet I should regret it, if I had to view the matter from this perspective alone.

Nathan, a paean in praise of Providence? Who, before Herr Mendelssohn, ever looked at it that way? The intent of the drama is strikingly and immediately manifest to any reader; [the intent of punishing without discrimination the pride and folly of all who imagine that *they know the only universal true way to God*; of stigmatizing as fanatics [Schwärmer] all those who as a consequence feel compelled to steer, yes, even force onto their own path, everyone who has missed it; of demonstrating most compellingly that all speculation about God and his universal governance is temerity, and that piety and wisdom lie alone in submission to Him.][1]

---

[1] Instead of [ ] the first edition has: "the intent of casting suspicion upon the spirit of all revelation, of presenting in a most unfavourable light, without discrimination, all religious systems *qua systems*. Once theism becomes a system and assumes *concrete form*, it is not exempted. The exception taken to other groups must also be taken to it. Indeed, theism must foster even greater fanaticism [fanatisch] than all religions based on tradition, because its self-conceit, arrogance, and contempt will be, in the

In fact, Spinoza urged such piety and wisdom far more heartily than did *Nathan*. He too worshipped a providence, even if to him it was the same as the very order of nature, which arises of necessity from its own eternal laws; he too related everything to God, *the One who alone IS*, and he saw the highest good in the recognition of the Infinite and in the love of Him above all things. He exclaims in his *Tractatus*:

> Eh, proh dolor! res eo jam pervenit, ut, qui aperte fatentur, se Dei ideam non habere, et Deum non nisi per res creatas (quarum causas ignorant) cognoscere, non erubescant Philosophos Atheismi accusare.
> [= Alas! it has come to this! those who openly admit to having no idea of God and to knowing God only through created things (the causes of which they do not know) do not blush to accuse philosophers of atheism]
> (*Tract. theol.- polit.*, C. II, p. 16)

Lessing published the first half of his *Education of the Human Race* before his *Nathan* and simultaneously with the *Fragments*; the booklet did not meet with Mendelssohn's approval and he rushes over it in his *Morgenstunden* as over hot coals. In my first letter to Mendelssohn I had discussed more specifically § 73 of that work and given that passage its proper interpretation. Once one follows the direction I pointed out, the whole essay, thought through with such profundity, so clearly demonstrates the correctness of my interpretation that I need not waste a single word over it with people well-versed in such things. I indicated briefly at an earlier point how Mendelssohn tried to set things straight with a contrived explanation that sought to redress the matter. He proved to our friend Lessing that *One cannot be All* because *One is not two* and *two is not One* - Lessing had not thought of that; not thought that, if self-consciousness is God's attribute as it is our's, as individual beings, God himself must then be an individual thing as well and one is bound to ascribe to him an extramundane existence (his infinity being presupposed); this theory invalidates the whole

---

nature of things, boundless. - Hence, away with concrete forms! Let this principle alone prevail: *the best man always has the best religion also*. - 'All speculation *about* God is temerity and folly, submission to him, piety and wisdom.'"

Hen kai Pan: this is the lesson Mendelssohn administers to Lessing, and the contrite sinner goes forth, beshamed and speechless.[1]

Mendelssohn could well have reprimanded Lessing on many other counts. In truth, it cannot be denied that the man had gone considerably far afield. For right in the same *Education of the Human Race* he says [§§ 33, 75,77, etc.] ....

(...)

The very idea of *doing things by halves* was an impossibility for Lessing, and he was no great admirer of those who could. A statement to this effect, notable in more than one respect, is found in his essay on *Wissowatius* [= *Werke*, VII, 222]. There he writes of Leibniz who is speaking about Locke: "Leibniz did not see Locke as one was wont to regard him: Inclinavit ad Socinianos, quorum *paupertina* semper fuit de Deo et mente philosophia [= Locke had a weakness for the Socinians whose philosophy of God and the human mind was *shallow* from the start]. Was it the shallower philosopher who created the Socinian, or the Socinian the shallower philosopher? Or is it that very shallowness of mind which results in one's so readily doing things by halves in both theology and philosophy?"

An upright person *may keep silent*; the wise person *must* often do so; but lie, one neither may nor must; never subordinate truth to his deceptive wisdom nor to his will, however pure he keep it; never undertake to promote by deceit what he thinks is *good* or *better*. It takes nothing less than the arrogance of Satan to exhalt ourselves above God's ways and arbitrarily to take into our own hands a truth that is not ours. As God is my witness I swear that these sentiments were Lessing's very own; that he despised and hated nothing more than that self-conceit which would set out to promote knowledge and happiness through force or fraud. The sheer madness of such an enterprise roused his scorn; its immorality [Ungerechtigkeit], his hatred.

---

[1] The first edition adds: "O, my fellowmen! Can you fault me because the pen in my hand trembles with reluctance at writing this? Indeed I shall repress it, this bitter reluctance; I shall keep silent about what is turning my stomach at this very moment."

Lessing's method is not to be confused with its polar opposite; there is a clear distinction between the two. For what greater contrast can there be than that between a wise humility which is "willing to put its own system aside", and stupid pride which insists upon enforcing its own system at all costs, introducing it everywhere, and tolerating none other beside it? This pride, since it takes its own opinion to be truth itself, considers itself to be reason *personified*, will brook no arguments and will always attempt only to *suppress* all arguments as being *base* and to curb all objections by any means whatsoever. The most distinguished talent, if it is useless for pride's purposes, will be stripped of its dignity, deprived of its good name and even extinguished, if that were possible. But yet, pride is totally unconscious of its own immorality; it rejoices in its own works because it knows one sole rule: the self-indulgence in its own private wisdom, and because its fanatical zeal, directed more to *cause* than to *person*, tramples justice and fairness under foot. Its lust for power, it sees as benevolence; its urge to oppress, as fatherly firmness -a regal virtue; its insight, as the opinion all must hold.

I come now to the accusations and reproaches made against meand which arise solely from the personage and philosophy of Herr Mendelssohn, and I know no more suitable place for a *restful pause*.[1]

The matter could certainly rest with this first session if my own self-defence were the *issue*. But this was hardly the case up to now and will be still less so as we proceed. While writing these pages, how often have I thought of a passage in Lessing's last letter to me, one with which I was sorely tempted to begin the present essay. "There is nothing," the worthy man wrote me on an occasion of some importance, "there is nothing of yours I would read with more pleasure than your own *apologia*." And he added encouraging words I would not think of quoting in a cause of lesser import than the present one: "To my mind, a man of your stamp is never

---

[1] The first edition adds: "While I am resting, let the reader occupy himself by reading anything else he might have at hand; thus both he and I will gain time to catch our breath and take in some fresh air."

in the wrong however much he appear so in the eyes of the whole world -*with which he should NOT*, I repeat: *not, have tangled."*

Are my opponents the kind of persons who care about *truth* and yield to *arguments?* This was precisely what exasperated them and now further inflames their anger with each new day. The more *my cause* reveals itself, by dint of elaborate arguments and proofs, as the best possible cause and *theirs* as the worst, the more furious they are and the more importunately they assail me, constantly devising fresh dodges and ploys. For, what on earth is it that they fear? In their hearts they foster that same valour, that same sense of honour which lends such courage to the Fier-en-fat in Voltaire's *Prodigal Son* where he cries:

> Soyons hardis, nous sommes dix contre un!
> [= Let's be bold, we are ten against one!]

And how much more must the courage of these latter-day Fier-en-fat surpass the courage of their *prototype* since they stand in *hundreds* against *me.* "They will talk on and on, refusing to be interrupted by me; they will talk on and on without caring whether or not our conversations mesh. They are wound up and now have to run down." [Lessing, *Axiomata*, X in *Werke* VIII, 150]

Let them! Not only am I, like Lessing, willing to be *out-shouted* but, very much unlike Lessing, I admit that I am willing to be *out-written.* The more they write and out-write me, the more they will lay bare their hearts' secrets; and the more the threads of a *hyper-crypto-Jesuitism* will emerge (a real one, not an *imaginary* one or one only fabricated for the purpose of covering their own widespread smuggling) and the threads of a *philosophical popery*; in *untold multifarious convolutions* they will expose to view *how far these threads reach.* I have no fear that this warning will prejudice my own cause. That "genus irritabile hominum, suique impotens" [= irascible species of men, lacking in all self-control], may indeed experience momentary shocks, but it cannot contain itself. One can take a chance by counting on their vanity and vindictiveness. Instead of falling back, they will run "and blindly throw themselves onto the point of the spear."

How much in this respect the short span of less than three months has taught us! How crystal-clear it became that philosophical dogmatism and fractiousness are no less hot-tempered, contagious, pompous, and bombastic than priestly breaches! How striking that fanaticism made them even more unjust, malicious and cruel; superstition, even more blind and stubborn, than is the case with the priests. - What slanders were not directed at me? Slanders Lessing with good reason calls "assassination". [*Axiomata*, Introd. in *Werke* VIII, 130] How they *twisted* my words and *falsified* my language in every which way!

"I blasphemed against reason"--because I assert that, according to the doctrine of the theists, it can neither demonstrate apodictically the existence of God nor satisfactorily refute the objections to it. They claim I said therewith "that all philosophy leads to atheism" (Nicolai). I am "a fanatic and intend to promote blind faith or even faith in miracles," because I affirm that one can only *believe* in God and establish oneself in this faith through *practice* alone.

What? *that* is the reason why? And Kant, who has been teaching that same thing for more than six years, has not blasphemed against reason? Kant is *not* a fanatic [Schwärmer] and is *not* trying to promote blind faith or faith in miracles?

Take up the *Critique of Pure Reason* and read there....

[= quotations from Kant follow, also from Hemsterhuis]

(...)

The shouts of these men in praise and defence of reason can be in part quite innocent. They actually believe *that their opinion is reason and reason their opinion*. There is no point in calling them madmen [Schwärmer] since madness [Schwärmerei] is only exaggerated *enthusiasm* [Enthusiasmus] - which does presuppose a real object. An enthusiast for an un-real object, for a non-being, is *not* labelled a madman, but a mere day-dreamer [Phantast]. This is the true name for that species: they are *day-dreamers*. If it happens that a zealot's ardour for a phantom object inflames him to the point of preaching his own truth and miracles, even to preaching his personal religion *wherein alone salvation lies*, then he is said to be driven by *fanaticism* [Fanatismus].

"By their fruits ye shall know them."

If these gentlemen had any insight into the *nature* of reason, how could they give way to those superstitious fears which are, after vanity and selfishness, the direct causes of intolerance and persecution? If they loved truth, how could they wish to wall it up within the narrow confines of their temples, wish to bring it under the sway of a priestly caste? But Reason, for them, is merely the image of the idol to which they make sacrifice - in any other form, an abomination; and they themselves nail it to the cross.

The cause of this dreadful derangement is that [they mistake the truth, which they perceive only *subjectively*, for the *objectively* known truth; they take it indeed][1] to be the only one and even confuse it with reason itself; or, as I have just said and take pleasure in repeating: they take their opinion to be reason and reason to be their opinion. In truth THEY are the people who test reason by *faith* and according to that faith alone affirm or deny reason - otherwise knowing nothing of it, caring neither for its nature nor for its requirements. By means of such a hypostatized truth then, the either received or self-made system rises out of all proportion and self-conceit utters prophecies which control all things and cannot be controlled by anything, prophecies which hold the spirit captive, seduce and lead the conscience astray.

(...)

I know what is in store for me. I stand alone against a whole host and sheep will follow sheep. It won't take very much to bring down completely someone who is already so low. Who will respect me then? Surely no one but he who is taken in by appearances. One need only examine my works to discover at once that I am not up to my subject, that I never pored over it, never researched sources; that I was still less familiar with its peculiar implications. I cannot even read properly, for if I knew how to read, to retain, and to reflect, would it not stand to reason that I would have the *right* faith, that I would acknowledge the *authentic church*? And

---

[1] The first edition has instead of [ ]: "they have the notion of an objective truth which they consider...."

write? Yes! I can phrase *words nicely*, but *write?* God save us from such discourse as that!

That is how things stand with me; and that is how things *will continue* to stand with me; thus I shall be to the image of [their] truth *which is prudent* [weise]. And if I, *just as I am*, am *catalogued* in each new issue of Herr Nicolai's *paraphrasings of the general book-fair brochure*, at every opportune or inopportune moment, *with* or *without* dignity, covertly and overtly, - and if the whole fraternity of journals and newspapers re-echo it, then who will not understand in the end, recognize, and *pay tribute alone* to the truth *which is prudent!*

I have all the more reason to make use of this one moment when I might still be heard.

I demanded strictest examination, *inexorable* justice, and I demand them anew.

Just compare now my defence with Mendelssohn's accusations and with the essays of those who support them, and judge how I would have fared, had I been guilty of something; had we been afforded *proofs* instead of inventions, calumnies, and vile bullying! Were *my* cause the cause of my adversaries - merciful God! I shudder at the thought!

Just let them go ahead and triumph over me! It is enough that they cannot triumph over my cause. It is enough that this very cause has taken a turn which could not be more instructive. The less I worked at it, the purer is my joy; and in all events the more perfect my peace will be.

[the work ends with a quotation from Lavater.]

BIBLIOGRAPHY

Editions of Lessing's Works

Sämtliche Schriften. Ed. by K. Lachmann; 3rd edition by Fr. Muncker. Stuttgart/Berlin/Leipzig 1886-1924. 23 vols. (referred to as Lachmann-Muncker or *LM*)

Gesammelte Werke. Ed. by P. Rilla. Berlin/Weimar 1954-1958. 1968[2]. 10 vols. (referred to as *GW*)

Lessings Werke. Ed. by K. Wölfel. Frankfurt 1967. 3 vols.

Werke. Ed. by H.G. Göpfert et al. München 1970-1979. 8 vols. (referred to as *Werke*)

Gesammelte Werke. Berlin/Weimar: Aufbau Verlag 1981-. 12 vols.

Werke und Briefe. Ed. by W. Barner et al. Deutscher Klassiker Verlag (Insel/Suhrkamp) 1985-. 12 vols.

Other Editions and Sources

F.H. Jacobi, *Werke*. Ed. by Fr. Roth and Fr. Köppen. Leipzig 1812-1825. 6 vols. Repr. Darmstadt 1968. Vol. 4 in 3 Parts (1819) is used here.

F.H. Jacobi, *Aus F.H. Jacobi's Nachlaß*. Ed. by R. Zoeppritz and W. Engelmann. Leipzig 1869. 2 vols.

F.H. Jacobi, *Briefwechsel*. Ed. by M. Brüggen and W. Sudhof. Stuttgart/Bad Cannstadt 1981- .

M. Mendelssohn, *Gesammelte Schriften*. Jubiläumsausgabe. Ed. by A. Altmann et al. Stuttgart/Bad Cannstadt:
Vol. 3,2, 1974 (ed. L. Strauss): *Morgenstunden* and *An die Freunde Lessings*.
Vol. 8, 1983: *Jerusalem oder über religiöse Macht und Judentum*.
Vol. 12,2, 1976: *Briefwechsel* II.2 (Jan. 1771 to Dec. 1780).
Vol. 13, 1977: *Briefwechsel* III (Jan. 1781 to end Dec. 1785).

R. Daunicht, ed., *Lessing im Gespräch*. München 1971.

H. Scholz, ed., *Die Hauptschriften zum Pantheismusstreit zwischen Jacobi und Mendelssohn*. Berlin 1916.

H.S. Reimarus, *Apologie oder Schutzschrift für die vernünftigen Verehrer Gottes*. G. Alexander, Ed., 2 vols. Hamburg 1972.

J.W. Goethe, *Dichtung und Wahrheit*. In *Goethes Werke*. Vol. X. München 1981.

Goethes Werke, Sect. IV, Vol. 23. Weimar 1900.

G.W.F. Hegel, *Sämtliche Werke*. Jubiläumsausgabe. Vol. 19. Stuttgart, 1959.

C. Middleton, ed., *J.W. von Goethe: Selected Poems*. Boston 1983.

General

E. Bahr, E.P. Harris and L.G. Lyon, eds., *Humanität und Dialog. Lessing und Mendelssohn in neuer Sicht*. Supplement to the *Lessing Yearbook*. Detroit/München 1982.

W. Barner, G. Grimm et al., *Lessing: Epochen, Werk, Wirkung*. München 1981[4].

W. Barner and A.M. Reh, eds., *Nation und Gelehrtenrepublik. Lessing im Europäischen Zusammenhang*. Supplement to the *Lessing Yearbook*. Detroit 1984.

G. and S. Bauer, eds., *G.E. Lessing.* "Wege der Forschung" 211. Darmstadt 1968.

K. Briegleb, *Lessings Anfänge 1742-1746.* Frankfurt 1971.

K.S. Guthke, *Lessing.* Stuttgart 1979.

E.P. Harris and R.E. Schade, eds., *Lessing in heutiger Sicht.* Bremen/Wolfenbüttel 1977.

G. Hartung, ed., *Beiträge zur Lessing-Konferenz 1979.* Halle 1979.

D. Hildebrandt, *Lessing: Biographie einer Emanzipation.* München 1979.

Lessing und die Zeit der Aufklärung. Göttingen 1968.

Lessing Yearbook [LY]. München 1969-1979; Detroit 1980- .

P. Rilla, *Lessing und sein Zeitalter.* Berlin 1958. 1968².

E. Schmidt, *Lessing: Geschichte seines Lebens und seiner Schriften.* 3 vols. Berlin 1884-1892.

G. Schulz, ed., *Lessing und der Kreis seiner Freunde.* Heidelberg 1985.

Seifert, *Lessing-Bibliographie.* Berlin/Weimar 1973.

M. Vanhelleputte, ed., "G.E. Lessing und die Freiheit des Denkens", *Tijdschrift voor de Studie van de Verlichting en van het Vrije Denken* 10(1982) Nr. 1-3.

H.G. Werner, ed., *Lessing-Konferenz 1979.* 2 Teile. Halle 1980.

K. Wölfel, ed., *Lessings Leben und Werk in Daten und Bildern.* Frankfurt 1967.

Wolfenbütteler Studien zur Aufklärung (WSA). Heidelberg 1974- .

The Spinoza Conversations and Lessing's Spinozism

L. Althaus, "Vom 'toten Hunde' Spinoza und Lessings 'Atheismus'". *Studia Germanica Gandensia* 14(1973) 161-181.

A. Altmann, *Moses Mendelssohn. A Biographical Study.* University of Alabama Press 1973.

A. Altmann, "Lessing und Jacobi: Das Gespräch über den Spinozismus". *Lessing Yearbook* III, 1971, 25-70.

P. Bayle, *Dictionnaire historique et critique.* Rotterdam 1697. Basle 1738⁵. German translation 1741-1744.

D. Bell, *Spinoza in Germany from 1670 to the Age of Goethe.* London 1984.

H. Blumenberg, *Arbeit am Mythos.* Frankfurt 1984⁴.

K. Bohnen, "Aspekte marxistischer Lessing-Rezeption". *WSA* IX(1981) 115-130.

M. Bollacher, "Excurs: G.E. Lessing". *Der junge Goethe und Spinoza.* Tübingen 1969, pp. 194-234.

H. Fisher-Lamberg, *Der junge Goethe.* Bd. III. Berlin 1966.

W. Gericke, *Sechs theologische Schriften G.E. Lessings.* Berlin 1985.

K. Gründer and W. Schmidt-Biggemann, eds, *Spinoza in der Frühzeit seiner religiösen Wirkung. WSA* XII. Heidelberg 1984.

K.S. Guthke, "Lessing und das Judentum". *WSA* IV(1977) 229-271.

K.S. Guthke, "Lessing und das Judentum oder Spinoza absconditus". *Das Abenteuer der Literatur.* Bern 1981, pp. 123-143.

K. Hammacher, "Lessings Spinozismus aufgezeigt an seinem Beitrag zur Wandlung der philosophischen Grundfragen nach Gott, Freiheit und Unsterblichkeit in der Aufklärung" in Vanhelleputte, ed., [see above].

Th. Höhle, ed., *Lessing und Spinoza*. Halle 1982.

S. Kierkegaard, *Concluding Unscientific Postscript*. Princeton 1941.

A. Liepert, "Der Spinozismus Lessings". *Deutsche Z. für Philosophie* 27(1979) 59-70.

F. Regner, "Lessings Spinozismus". *ZThK* 68(1971) 351-375.

K. Rehorn, *G.E. Lessings Stellung zur Philosophie des Spinoza*. Frankfurt 1877.

H. Schultze, *Lessings Toleranzbegriff. Eine theologische Studie*. Göttingen 1969, pp. 107 ff.

R. Schwarz, "Lessings 'Spinozismus'". *ZThK* 65(1968) 271-290.

T.C. van Stockum, *Spinoza - Jacobi - Lessing*. Diss. Groningen 1916.

H. Timm, *Gott und die Freiheit. Studien zur Religionsphilosophie der Goethezeit*. Vol. 1: Die Spinozarenaissance. Frankfurt 1974.

On Jacobi

G. Baum, *Vernunft und Erkenntnis. Die Philosophie F.H. Jacobis*. Bonn 1969.

K. Hammacher, *Die Philosophie F.H. Jacobis*. München 1969.

K. Hammacher, ed., *F.H. Jacobi, Philosoph und Literat der Goethezeit*. Frankfurt 1971.

K. Homann, *F.H. Jacobis Philosophie der Freiheit*. München 1973.

L. Lévy-Bruhl, *La philosophie de Jacobi*. Paris 1894.

Lessing's Philosophy of Religion

H.E. Allison, *Lessing and the Enlightenment*. Ann Arbor 1966.

E.H. Amberg, "Lessings Gottesanschauung in heutiger Sicht". *ThLZ* 106(1981) 466-472.

E.A. Bergmann, *Hermaea. Studien zu G.E. Lessings theologischen und philosophischen Schriften*. Leipzig 1883.

M. Bollacher, *Lessing: Vernunft und Geschichte*. Tübingen 1978.

B. Bothe, *Glaube und Erkennen. Studie zur Religionsphilosophie Lessings*. Königstein 1972.

W. Dilthey, "G.E. Lessing". *Das Erlebnis und die Dichtung*. Leipzig/Berlin 1905, 1919[6], pp. 17-174.

W. Dilthey, "F.D.E. Schleiermacher". *Gesammelte Schriften* XV. Göttingen 1970, pp. 17-36.

M. Durzak, *Poesie und Ratio*. Bad Homburg 1970.

G. Fittbogen, *Die Religion Lessings*. Leipzig 1923.

I. Graham, *Goethe and Lessing. The Wellsprings of Creation*. New York 1973.

M. Haug, *Entwicklung und Offenbarung bei Lessing*. Gütersloh 1928.

P. Heller, *Dialectics and Nihilism*. University of Massachusetts Press 1966.

J. van den Hengel, "Reason and Revelation in Lessing's Enlightenment". *Eglise et théologie* 17(1986) 171-194.

I. Kant, "Was es heisst: Sich im Denken orientieren"? 1786. *Kants gesammelte Schriften* VIII. Berlin 1923, pp. 131-147.

A. Kenny, *Faith and Reason*. New York 1983.

G.E. Michalson,Jr., *Lessing's "Ugly Ditch": A Study of Theology and History*. Pennsylvania State University Press 1985.

W. Oelmüller, *Die unbefriedigte Aufklärung. Beiträge zu einer Theorie der Moderne von Lessing, Kant und Hegel*. Frankfurt 1969.

H.E. Pagliaro, ed., *Irrationalism in the 18th Century*. Cleveland 1972.

G. Pons, *G.E. Lessing et le christianisme*. Paris 1964.

G. Pons, "Lessings Auseinandersetzung mit der Apologetik". *ZThK* 77(1980)381-411.

A. Schilson, "G.E. Lessing und die Theologie. Zum Stand der Forschung". *Theologie und Philosophie* 47(1972) 409-428.

A. Schilson, *Geschichte im Horizont der Vorsehung*. Mainz 1974.

A. Schilson, *Lessings Christentum*. Göttingen 1980.

J. Schneider, *Lessings Stellung zur Theologie vor der Herausgabe der Wolfenbütteler Fragmente*. 's-Gravenhage 1953.

C. Schwarz, *G.E. Lessing als Theologe*. Halle 1854.

H. Thielicke, *Offenbarung, Vernunft und Existenz. Studien zum Religionsphilosophie Lessings*. Gütersloh 1957[4].

L.P. Wessell, *G.E. Lessing's Theology. A Reinterpretation*. Den Haag/Paris 1977.

Lessing's Aesthetics and Criticism

K. Bohnen, *Geist und Buchstabe. Zum Prinzip des kritischen Verfahrens in Lessings literarästhetischen und theologischen Schriften*. Köln/Wien 1974.

J. Desch, "Lessings Dramaturgie und Religionsphilosophie in ihrem Zusammenhang". Diss. Marburg 1951.

J. Desch, "Lessings 'poetische' Antwort auf die Reimarusfragmente". *H.S. Reimarus (1694-1768) ein "bekannter Unbekannter" der Aufklärung in Hamburg.* Göttingen 1973, pp. 75-95.

H. Göbel, *Bild und Sprache bei Lessing.* München 1971.

E. Heftrich, *Lessings Aufklärung. Zu den theologischphilosophischen Spätschriften.* Frankfurt 1978.

V. Nölle, *Subjektivität und Wirklichkeit in Lessings dramatischen und theologischen Werk.* Berlin 1977.

J.G. Robertson, *Lessing's Dramatic Theory.* New York 1965[2]

V.A. Rudowski, *Lessing's Aesthetics in nuce: An Analysis of the May 26, 1769 Letter to Nicolai.* University of North Carolina Press 1981.

A. Schilson, "Lessing's 'Kritik der Vernunft'". *Theol. Quartalschrift* 162(1982) 24-30.

H. Timm, "Eine theologische Tragikomödie. Lessings Neuinszenierung der Geistesgeschichte". *Zs. für Religions- und Geistes-Geschichte* 34(1982) 1-17.

TABLE 1. From Lessing's Life and Works

1729	January 22, born in Kamenz, third of twelve children, son of a Lutheran pastor.
1741-1746	Classical education in Meißen. First essays in poetry.
1746-1748	Begins study of theology at the university of Leipzig; then interested in philology, philosophy, medicine, archeology. Literary activity and introduction to theatre life. *Der junge Gelehrte* [1747]. Aims at becoming a "German Molière".
1748-1755	Berlin [1748-1751] and Wittenberg; lives as writer, journalist and critic. Influence of P. Bayle. Friendship with Nicolai, von Kleist, Gleim; with Mendelssohn, with whom he co-authors *Pope ein Metaphysiker!* [1755]. *Die Juden* [1749]. *Der Freigeist* [1749]. *Gedanken über die Herrnhuter* [1750]. *Schriften* in six parts [including fables, "Rettungen", *Miß Sara Sampson...*] [1753-1755]. *Das Christentum der Vernunft* [1751/52]. *Die Religion* [1753].
1755-1760	Leipzig and Berlin. Travels to Hamburg, Amsterdam. Correspondence with Mendelssohn and Nicolai. Translations. Study of history of literature. *Literaturbriefe....*

1760-1767   Breslau [secretary of a Prussian general for five years] and Berlin.
Study of the Church Fathers and of Spinoza.
Über die Entstehung der geoffenbarten Religion [1760 or 1763/64].
Von der Art und Weise der Fortpflanzung und Ausbreitung der christlichen Religion [after 1760].
Über die Wirklichkeit der Dinge außer Gott [1763].
Laokoon [1766].
Minna von Barnhelm [1767].

1767-1770   Hamburg, theatre critic at the national theatre.
Hamburger Dramaturgie [1767-1768].
Briefe antiquarischen Inhalts [1769].
Meets with pastor Goeze, families Reimarus and König.

1770-1781   Wolfenbüttel, librarian at the Herzog-August-Bibliothek; pamphleteer.
Berangerius Turonensis [1770].
Emilia Galotti [1772].
Allowed to publish [without censorship] a series, "Zur Geschichte und Literatur. Aus den Schätzen der Herzoglichen Bibliothek zu Wolfenbüttel".
Publishes fragments of Reimarus' *Apologie* [1774-1778].
Marriage with Eva König [October 1776]. Son and wife die fifteen months later.
Controversy with Goeze [1778] and other theologians. Lessing again submitted to censorship.
Ernst und Falk [1778-1780].
Nathan der Weise [1779].
Die Erziehung des Menschengeschlechtes [1780].
Die Religion Christi [1780].
Conversations with Jacobi [July and August 1780].
Dies on February 15, 1781 in Braunschweig.

TABLE 2. Main figures around the Spinoza conversations

B. de Spinoza	1632-1677
G.W. Leibniz	1646-1716
P. Bayle	1647-1706
Count of Shaftesbury	1671-1713
C. Wolff	1679-1754
H.S. Reimarus	1694-1768
S.J. Baumgarten	1706-1757

G.E. Lessing	1729-1781
M. Mendelssohn	1729-1786
F.H. Jacobi	1743-1819

E.C. von Kleist	1715-1759 poet, Prussian officer
J.M. Goeze	1717-1786 pastor in Hamburg
J.W.L. Gleim	1719-1803 poet
F. Hemsterhuis	1722-1790 philosopher and archeologist
I. Kant	1724-1804
J.A.H. Reimarus	1729-1814 son of H.S. Reimarus, for many years Lessing's physician
J.G. Hamann	1730-1788
C.F. Nicolai	1733-1811 publisher and writer
E. Reimarus	1735-1805 daughter of H.S. Reimarus
K.G. Lessing	1740-1812 brother of G.E.L.
J.G. Herder	1744-1803
J.W. Goethe	1749-1832

TABLE 3. Others indirectly related to the conversations

Voltaire	1694-1778
J.C. Edelmann	1698-1767
J.F. Jerusalem	1709-1789
J.D. Schumann	1714-1787
D.W. Winckelmann	1717-1768
J.D. Michaelis	1717-1791
C. Bonnet	1720-1793
C.F. Voß	1722-1795
J.S. Semler	1725-1791
C.W.F. Walch	1726-1784
Eva König-Lessing	1736-1778
J.C. Lavater	1741-1799
J.J. Engel	1741-1802
A. von Hennings	1746-1826
K.W. Jerusalem	1747-1772
A.A. von Gallitzin	1748-1806

INDEX